An Anatomy of the Financial Crisis

An Anatomy of the Financial Crisis

Blowing Tumbleweed

When institutions are too big to FRAME!
What lessons can we learn and are we capable of learning them?

Nashwa Saleh, CFA

ANTHEM PRESS
LONDON · NEW YORK · DELHI

Anthem Press
An imprint of Wimbledon Publishing Company
www.anthempress.com

This edition first published in UK and USA 2010
by ANTHEM PRESS
75-76 Blackfriars Road, London SE1 8HA, UK
or PO Box 9779, London SW19 7ZG, UK
and
244 Madison Ave. #116, New York, NY 10016, USA

British Library Cataloguing in Publication Data
A catalogue record for this book is available from the British Library.

Library of Congress Cataloging in Publication Data
A catalog record for this book has been requested.

ISBN-13: 978 0 85728 961 2 (Pbk)
ISBN-10: 0 85728 961 6 (Pbk)

ISBN-13: 978 0 85728 992 6 (eBook)
ISBN-10: 0 85728 992 6 (eBook)

CONTENTS

LIST OF FIGURES

ACKNOWLEDGMENTS AND DISCLAIMER

To my parents, Nabila El Haddad and Sherif Saleh, and my uncle Saad El Haddad. May they rest in peace.

I am grateful for all I have learned from my professors and work colleagues. I could not have worked on this book without the knowledge they passed on. I would specifically like to thank Professors Viral Acharya, Richard Portes, Andrew Scott and Suleyman Başak of London Business School, Professor Gulnur Muradoglu and Professor Andrew Clare, Dr Barbara Casu of Cass Business School, Mr Gabriele Stern of the Bank of England, Professors Ali Hadi, Medhat Hassanein and Hazem Yassin of The American University in Cairo (AUC), Mr John O'Keefe of the Federal Deposit Insurance Corporation (FDIC), Dr James Irving, London School of Economics (LSE), Mr Tarek Osman of NW11 Partners and Mr Gertjan Koomen of Sothic Capital Management, Mr Tim Turner, director, Private Sector Department, African Development Bank (AfDB), Mr Tarek Amer, chairman of the National Bank of Egypt and Mr Husssein Choucri, chairman of HC Securities & Investments.

I am especially grateful to Professor Andrew Clare of Cass Business School for suggesting the 'An Anatomy of the Crisis' part of the title of the book and to Professor Richard Portes whom I first heard coin the term 'too big to manage' in September 2009, which channelled my thoughts in the direction of a broader too big to FRAME concept.

The views expressed are entirely my own and are not linked in any way to bodies the author has engaged with in any working arrangement or affiliation, whether existing or in the past.

PREFACE

In 2007, Goldman Sachs revenues booked USD46 billion of net revenues, of which USD31 billion came from trading and principal investments (68%). The USD46 billion of net revenues this one investment bank booked was greater than the GDP of more than 100 developing countries, as noted by the renowned financial historian Professor Niall Ferguson in his *The Ascent of Money: A Financial History of the World*. What kind of activities did the bank engage in to generate this much in trading revenues? What kind of commissions did it charge on the transactions it undertook and how big were these transactions to turn such a profit? If, for example, we assume a commission of 1% of notional value of transactions and that it was only trading, it would give USD3.1 trillion in dealings – greater than the GDP of 27 out of the 30 Organization for Economic Co-Operation and Development (OECD) countries in 2007! OECD countries captured 74% of global GDP in 2007; so what kind of leverage went into these transactions? If we assume the USD31 billion all came from proprietary trading and that these investments returned 10%, this would mean a notional amount invested of USD310 billion on an 'all-equity basis'. But given close to zero interest rates, what investments returned 10% in the investment universe available to banks and to all other investors for that matter? A similar picture can be presented for all of the 'big boys' who were doing well prior to the onset of the financial crisis. So what were they doing? How can any institution of this size be managed? How can it be regulated? How do you deal with its failure? Goldman Sachs and many other dream employers of generations of graduates, have simply become Too big to Fail, to Regulate, to Audit, to Manage and to Evaluate. **In other words they have become too big to FRAME**!

From an analytical perspective, when the current crisis began is debatable. Some say as early as the third quarter of 2006 when the US housing market started turning (Acharya 2009) or in April 2007 when specialized subprime mortgage lender New Century filed for bankruptcy after having disbursed some USD60 billion in mortgage loans in 2006. In a speech in early 2007, Ben Bernanke acknowledged problems with the US subprime housing market and put a price tag of USD50 billion to USD100 billion of estimated losses on the crisis. In the same speech, he assured the market that this was a fraction of the US household USD57 trillion or so net worth.

The confidence crisis, the drying up of liquidity, the shift in risk premiums, the collapse of segments of the securitization market, bank and insurance failures and the complete mayhem in the global financial system that followed was not foreseen. So how did a disconnect in a sub-segment of a market in one country, the US, and individual too big to **FRAME** institutions snowball into a full-blown global financial catastrophe of an estimated USD3.4 trillion in direct write-down losses and an unfathomable iceberg of indirect costs? *A crisis which will continue blowing tumbleweed or maybe tangleweed in the way of global policy makers and bankers for at least another two decades?* This reader aims at addressing the question by discussing, in an analytical manner, highlights of:

    i. the big picture and the too big to FRAME issue;
   ii. the evolution of the structure of the global financial sector pre-crisis and systemic hot spots;
  iii. crisis unravelling, key events and turning points;
  iv. systemic and institutional crisis cost;
   v. regulatory regimes and response to the crisis; and finally
  vi. the way forward, macroprudential analysis and early warning systems for fragility and crises; and
 vii. the regulatory tumbleweed, or is it tangleweed, that will continue to plague regulators for decades as a result.

The objective of this discussion is to help 'summarize' the crisis in a holistic way, bringing to light a new perspective on each of the issues while simultaneously providing a solid platform for those wishing to research any of the sub-topics independently. It comprises a clear synthesis and original analysis of the various factors that led to the financial crisis of 2007–10 and beyond; a comprehensive coverage scope to date in terms of market, country and instruments; useful supervisory architecture insights and regulatory implications; and food for thought on outlook for the real economy and emerging markets. It is designed to be accessible to a beginner, intermediate or advanced readership.

ACRONYMS

ABCP	asset-backed commercial paper
ADIA	Abu Dhabi Investment Authority
AfDB	African Development Bank
ALM	Asset-liability management
ARMs	Adjustable rate mortgages
ASMI	All-the-Same-Market Composite Index
AUC	American University in Cairo
BCBS	Basle Committee on Banking Supervision
BIS	Bank for International Settlements
BRICs	Brazil, Russia, India, China
BRT	binary recursive trees
CAMELS	Capital adequacy, asset quality, management, efficiency, liquidity and sensitivity
CDS	credit default swap
CEE	Central and Eastern Europe
CEMEA	Central and Eastern Europe, the Middle East and Africa
CGFS	Committee on the Global Financial System
CMBOR	Centre for Management Buyout Research
CPSS	Committee on Payment and Settlement Systems
DIFC	Dubai International Financial Centre
EBA	European Banking Authority
ECB	European Central Bank
EIOPA	European Insurance and Occupational Pensions Authority
EMH	efficient market hypothesis
ESA	European Securities Authority
EWS	early warning systems
FDIC	Federal Deposit Insurance Corporation
FHLBs	Federal Home Loan Banks
FSB	Financial Stability Board
FSI	Financial Stability Institute
GFSR	Global Financial Stability Report

GSEs	Government Sponsored Enterprises
HRE	Hypo Real Estate
IADI	International Association of Deposit Insurers
IAIS	International Association of Insurance Supervisors
IASB	International Accounting Standards Board
IIF	Institute of International Finance
IMF	International Monetary Fund
IOSCO	International Organization of Securities Commissions
LATW	lean-against-the-wind
LCFI	Large and Complex Financial Institution
LIAR loans	self-certified loans
LOLR	lender of last resort
LSE	London School of Economics
LTROs	longer-term refinancing operations
LTV	Loan to Value Ratio
NINJA	No-income-no-job-loans
OECD	Organisation for Economic Co-Operation and Development
OTC	over-the-counter
PDCF	Primary Dealer Credit Facility
PIGS	Portugal, Italy, Greece and Spain
RoE	return on equity
SIR	single-integrated regulator
SIVs	Structured Investment Vehicles
SPE	special purpose entity
SSA	Sub-Saharan Africa
SWFs	Sovereign wealth funds
TAF	Term Auction Facility
TSLF	Term Securities Lending Facility
WB	World Bank
WEF	World Economic Forum

Chapter 1

THE CRISIS AND THE TOO BIG TO FRAME PROBLEM: THE BIG PICTURE FIRST

How did a dislocation in a sub-segment of a market in one country, the US, snowball into a full-blown global systemic financial catastrophe with an estimated USD3.4 trillion in direct write-down losses and an unfathomable iceberg of indirect costs, including an estimated USD10.2 trillion of global GDP opportunity losses? The answer to these questions lies in an intricate set-up of inter-linkages and imbalance build-ups in the US and across the globe, amplified many times over by *leverage* and *poor governance and ethics* resulting in institutions that are too big to **FRAME**. *A true Turner Snowstorm where nothing comes to rest and all is siphoned in a spiral of a distant point in the horizon with unpredictable movements of snow and water. Think of the painting, think of how you feel looking at the distant point in the horizon where it all fades into ambiguity.*

This chapter attempts to build a BIG, clear picture of the crisis which will later be fleshed out in detail throughout the book. The chapter starts with a discussion of the preconditions and evolution of the structure of the pre-crisis global financial system and systemic hot spots. Then it presents a new mapping and interpretation of the various overlapping phases of the crisis and the systemic and institutional crisis cost by different players, in different domiciles and a global tally. It will also discuss the existing regulatory regime structures and how they responded to the crisis on a country and cross-border level, which systems and structures resulted in the least losses, the regulatory changes proposed, where we go from here, in addition to the road map ahead for macroprudential analysis and early warning systems (EWS) for financial fragility and crises. The chapter will provide a short discussion of minimum requirements needed for a robust EWS and explore meta-theories to use in guiding new EWS design given the failure of pre-existing systems in predicting the current crisis and thereby significantly increasing its costs. These pages will raise the following questions: What are the implications for regulation? Is it tumbleweed or is it tangleweed facing regulators? What is the critique of these proposed changes? How does the concept of too big to FRAME picture in all this? The details follow.

1.1 The Evolution of the Global Financial Sector Structure Pre-Crisis and Systemic Hot Spots

With a low interest rate environment, two main changes in financial player business models took place: a) a continuous search for yield and b) ever-increasing leverage, mainly in unregulated opaque OTC markets. The notional outstanding amount of derivatives was more than 10 times the global GDP in 2008. Securitization grew to represent a larger portion in bank wholesale funding and credit extension, capturing a little under a third of outstanding credit in the US, mostly linked to the housing sector. Europe, in contrast, relied on securitization to a limited extent (6% of total outstanding credit), but held a disproportionate share of risk, owning more than 72% of ABCP committed facilities globally. As the crisis unravelled, global banking sector capitalization collapsed to almost a third of what it was pre-crisis to USD2.6 trillion in March 2009.

1.1.1 Insurance Companies

Insurance companies heavily involved in the securitization market through the provision of credit enhancement (specifically in the US market which is comprised of 60% non-life activities versus only 40% of insurance activities related to life) guaranteed some *USD2.4 trillion* in asset-backed securities. When this market sub-segment began to collapse, a number of them lost their Triple-A status while insurance giant AIG had to be bailed out by the US government after booking losses to the tune of *USD100 billion* in 2008.

1.1.2 Non-Bank Financial Institutions

Pension fund assets sustained estimated losses of USD3.2 trillion (out of USD25 trillion estimated total assets), while the USD2.0 trillion hedge fund industry saw 62 funds collapse. Recent data on private equity activity shows 1H09 deals falling to almost a quarter of what they were in 1H08. Fannie Mae and Freddie Mac, US Government Sponsored Enterprises (GSEs), exposed to USD5.3 trillion of mortgage-related instruments, were taken over by the US government in September 2008. Structured Investment Vehicles (SIVs), a type of off-balance sheet special purpose entity (SPE) used by banks to raise cheap capital in the short-term money markets and seek yields in an opaque, unregulated manner, collectively held assets of USD300 billion at the beginning of 2007, of which less than USD50 billion was equity financed, and the majority were sponsored by US banks. Theoretically without recourse to their sponsors, these ended up being subsumed or fully merged with their sponsors as the crisis unravelled.

1.1.3 Roll-out of Basle II

Institutions adopting the new accord and the implementation of the various pillars meant that *bigger banks with more sophisticated risk management systems and greater risk exposures ended up holding less capital.* At the same time implementation of Pillar II supervisory tools lagged considerably.

1.1.4 Governance Issues

Governance issues specifically related to the US securitization market included No-Income-No-Job (NINJA) loans; Adjustable Rate Mortgages (ARMs); liar loans where borrowers self-certify their own submitted information – all selling at very low initial teaser rates; and the failure of the originate-and-distribute model.

1.1.5 No Credit-Risk Transfer

There was no credit-risk transfer, neither between different market players (banks, insurance companies and investors), nor to vehicles set up by their sponsors. *Banks were forced to take back around 95% of their own sponsored SIV assets, and held on-balance sheet pre-crisis around 40% of other SIVs of which they were not sponsors.*

1.2 Weak Capitalization, Excessive Leverage and Skewed Funding Structures

Weak capitalization and excessive leverage are major culprits in increasing bank fragility. My decomposition analysis of US, Euro and UK banks return on equity – using on-balance sheet data from Bankscope – in 1996 and 2007 shows that the increase in banking sector return on equity (RoE) over the period was predominantly a pure leverage play, where ROE = return on assets (RoA) x leverage. Had this increase in leverage not taken place, banking return on assets would have been much lower due to increased competition and smaller spreads. This is especially true for the UK, which saw leverage increase from 18x in 1996 to 28x in 2007.

As leverage normalizes to pre-crisis levels, and if we assume pre-crisis levels to be 25x, this would point to normalized post-crisis RoEs of around 14% across Europe, 12.1% for the US and 16.6% for the UK respectively. If we assume more aggressive deleveraging to only 10x, RoEs would fall to 6.6% in the US, 5.4% in Europe and 4.8% in the UK. This is proof that the shift in the banking industry is a structural one, with real impact on business models, and *not* a transitory shock after which we will return to pre-crisis norms. Moreover, this simulation does not take into account increased regulatory burdens, whether in the form of 'systemic taxes' or others. With lower profitability, it will take longer to build capital buffers.

The funding structure of banks over the same period reflects some core shifts, with deposits and short-term funding continuing to constitute a stable percentage of around two thirds of total balance sheet funding. However, the proportion of wholesale funding as a percentage of total deposits and short-term funding shows a massive shift, rising from 24% in the US in 1996, 7% in Europe and 29% in the UK to 40% and 19% in the US and Europe respectively in 2007 and a whopping 84% in the UK.

1.3 Global Imbalances: Systemic Significance of the US Too High

The systemic significance of the US in global equity capital markets in 2008 – (20% of total global equity market capitalization of USD59.8 trillion), global market share of securitizations (greater than 50%), banking sector capitalization (12% pre-crisis, 14% post-crisis), global insurance industry (around a third in terms of premiums), share of non-bank financial institutions and SIVs activities in the financial markets and money market funding as a percentage of total deposits and short-term funding being a hefty 40% – explains why and how the spillovers were transmitted and were of this magnitude.

1.4 Crisis Unravelling, Key Events and Turning Points

A massive build-up of imbalances in the US economy over the period from 2001–2007 on the back of extremely low policy rates can be identified as phase one or as a prelude to the current crisis which led to the development of an asset price boom and a credit boom – all aspects of economic activity simply became too big relative to the underlying fundamental economic muscle power.

This prelude is the only phase clearly distinct from what followed, with subsequent phases overlapping. As the US housing market turned, phase two of the crisis, the US subprime crisis (2006–2007 and beyond) unravelled: a segment of the subprime securitized mortgage loans with adjustable rates started to default, leading to the bankruptcy of two mortgage lenders – Ownit Mortgage Solutions at the end of 2006, followed by New Century Financial in April 2007. This was followed by the collapse in June 2007 of two highly leveraged Bear Stearns hedge funds. The events resemble the Florida Real Estate Craze of 1923 described in Burton Malkiel's *A Random Walk Down Wall Street* but with a modern twist – and far more dire consequences. He depicts the real estate asset bubble in Florida and the atmosphere of euphoria which led investors to wrongly assume 'that this market has no downside', the same argument on which all securitization products structured in the subprime market were based: that property prices would always rise. He gives the example of Palm Beach land bought for USD800,000 only to be resold one year later for USD1.5 million and another year later valued at USD4 million, with *one third* of Florida's population at the peak of the boom working as real estate agents. How many mortgage brokers in total were there at peak market growth prior to the crisis? And the modern twist? Florida is still one of the main problem-hit areas in regional real estate in the US. With today's financial innovation, in all problem regions in the US and elsewhere, instead of being able to see clearly who owns the real estate being sold, or the detailed cash flows from which the value of whatever securitized product you bought as an investor is derived, now it is all thrown in a 'pool' and out come 'tranches' of 'Triple A': credit enhanced securities, so there is no way of knowing exactly what you are paying for. As an investor, you naturally had confidence in the approval *stamp* by the rating agencies which in turn relied on *audit* firms to validate the accounts they based upon their credit rating decisions.

This was followed by phase three (September 2008 and beyond). On the heels of the bankruptcy of Lehman Brothers, what started as credit losses in one market sub-segment boiled over into a confidence crisis, shifting of risk premiums and in turn an almost complete drying up of liquidity and wholesale funding markets. This spiralled into self-fulfilling prophecies of asset sales to meet margin calls leading to more asset sales and value collapsed across all markets, resulting in US Bank and non-bank financial institutions (NBFI) failures. The 1980s movie *Rollover* starring Jane Fonda did a great job of describing a similar scenario, only in this movie it was the sudden withdrawal of all 'oil' or 'Arab' monies held at US banks and the impact of a liquidity 'siphon' on the market. The depiction was not far from what has happened over the past few years, again with the modern twist of an overlay of 'innovative financial instruments'.

Phase four covers the global bank and NBFI failures, which I define as starting in January 2008 following the collapse of Northern Rock in the UK. With their unsustainable business model, and being too big to **FRAME**, heavyweight players were starting to collapse.

Finally comes phase five. Because these individual players were too big to FRAME, there was a huge impact on global real macro performance, which

I define as starting in 2008 and beyond. A discussion of these phases is presented in Chapter 2 and a detailed timeline of crisis events in the US, UK, Europe and countries across the globe is presented in Appendix 1. Appendix 2 presents prior crises in recent history.

1.5 Systemic and Institutional Crisis Cost

How do we define the cost of crises in academic literature? And how big were previous crises in comparison to the current one with a total cost of around 25% of estimated global GDP in 2009? Davis & Karim (2003) identify cost of systemic crises as both *direct bailouts cost* and *indirect in terms of GDP costs*. Caprio and Klingebiel (1996) find bailouts cost on average 10% of GDP, with some crises much more costly like the Mexican Tequila Crisis (1994) which cost 20% of GDP and the Jamaican crisis (1996) which had a toll equivalent to 37% of GDP. According to an update from the IMF, world growth is projected to fall to a mere 0.5% percent, the lowest rate since World War II, with significant financial strains remaining acute. Cumulative (indirect) output losses over 2008–10 are projected at around 5% of global output (USD10.2 trillion if we apply the rate to IMF global output estimates).

The IMF's total estimate of direct losses in the form of write-downs was revised significantly upwards in April 2009 to USD4.0 trillion (from USD1.45 trillion in April 2008 and USD945 million in January 2008) and down again in October 2009 to USD3.4 trillion. Actual losses globally realized thus far by financial institutions amounted to USD1.9 trillion (USD760 billion in September 2008, of which USD580 billion were by banks). Are we to see the rest of these losses materialize?

If we classify the losses into: i) losses which have already been realized; (ii) losses still to be realized, *have been estimated in magnitude* but their timing is uncertain; and (iii) losses which are unknown in size and are yet to materialize at an unknown date, it is this last leg which creates the greatest uncertainty and comprises the biggest risk of further self-fulfilling losses being realized. These different categories point to a potential hidden 'iceberg' of losses yet to be realized. Briefing reports of the Macroprudential Unit at the Central Bank of Egypt identified as *early as August 2007* some of the potential spillovers into other credit market sub-segments and to other financial sector players.

The Bank of England's Financial Stability Report of April 2007 was spot on in quantifying potential losses to the banking sector to the tune of GBP60 billion, or 30% to 35% of its capitalization. The estimate presented for six different stress factors in disaggregation, accurately capturing first order effects.

1.6 Outlook for Write-Downs, Provisioning, Capital Raisings and Refinancing Needs

The outlook for further write-downs and loss provisioning by region shows that the bulk of these are yet to be realized for the UK and the Eurozone (only 40% of needed write-downs booked), while the US is ahead in the cycle (60% of needed write-downs booked).

According to the IMF's Global Financial Stability Report (GFSR) in October of 2009, major global banking players had capital injections of some USD930 billion from crisis inception to 2Q09. The IMF estimates that in 2010, to shore up capital ratios and support modest credit growth a further USD180 billion on the low-end, USD530 billion in the mid-range and USD670 billion on the high-end will be needed, based on three scenarios of different target minimum capital ratios.

The IMF estimates that over 2009 and the first quarter of 2010, the largest global banks face funding needs of over *USD700 billion*. Eurozone banks still rely heavily on wholesale funding markets and thus will face huge refinancing requirements in 2009 and 2010. For the UK, according to analyses undertaken by the Bank of England and Fathom Consulting, funding needs are forecast to peak in 2011 and 2012, with some GBP650 billion plus in net liabilities to be refinanced based on maturity ladders of existing funding.

1.7 Outlook for the Real Economy

1.7.1 Credit Crunch the Musical?

On a small stage in Covent Garden in 2008 an amateur group of performers, part of Pineapple Dance Studios, presented a musical capturing the impact of the credit crunch on a TV production company and its employees. It was a light, funny affair, but at the end of the day was spot on in describing on a microlevel what happens in a 'credit crunch' state, which boils down to a simple question of 'how are we going to pay next month's rent'? or, put differently, 'how do we address our financing needs in near, medium and long terms?' In academia, Demirgüç-Kunt and Detragiache (2005) identify the impact of banking crises with respect to the real economy in the form of a credit crunch hypothesis where markets are starved for credit following a crisis resulting in output losses. This has found strong empirical support in Lindgren et al (1996), Kaminsky and Reinhart (1999) and Eichengreen and Rose (1998). They find that more financially dependent sectors lose about 1% of growth in each crisis year compared to less financially dependent sectors. A study by Demirgüç-Kunt, Detragiache and Gupta (2000) finds that growth of both deposits and credit slows down substantially and banks reallocate their asset portfolio away from loans. This seems to be applicable to the current crisis. Thus, both theory and empirical findings indicate that in times of financial stress, banks prefer cash instruments and reserves to traditional extension of credit and other products to the market. The sharp drop in the ratio of interbank lending to total bank reserves in the US and the drastic fall in loan multiplier (loans divided by bank reserves) over January 1999-May 2009 are evidence of this. Think of how people stored money in medieval times: in silver and gold like the Spanish conquistadors; in camel herds in the Arabian peninsula; in the form of cow herds in Africa (the cultural significance of which is demonstrated in Alexander McCall Smith's insightful and funny 'No. 1 Detective Agency' series); or as coinage in whatever form, hidden under a mattress, in a palm tree-lined courtyard, in dome- and poetry-overlaid houses with gilded coffered ceilings or under floor tiles in the 'harem' rooms.

1.7.2 Lower Potential Output

The IMF estimates that over the 2008–10 period, global output, as a result of the financial crisis, will be potentially USD10.2 trillion lower than what it would have been had there been no crisis. As Niall Ferguson notes in his *Ascent of Money*, in the afterword on the 'Descent of Money', Former Federal Reserve Governor Frederic Mishkin said, 'the financial system [is] the brain of the economy... It acts as a coordinating mechanism that allocates capital to businesses and households. If capital goes to the wrong uses or does not flow at all, the economy will operate inefficiently, and ultimately economic growth will be low.' This is very true: poor intermediation leads to potential output losses and to actual realized losses.

1.7.3 Demand Side Rebalancing and Chimerica

Economists in the industry were forecasting a tectonic shift in the balance of global financial power, with China surpassing the US by 2050: after all with a population of 1.3 billion (greater than the 30 OECD countries combined and a *fifth* of the global population), its GDP was only USD3.4 trillion, coming in third compared to the OECD group members (the US at USD14 trillion, Japan USD4.4 trillion and Germany at USD3.3 trillion in 2007). More importantly, China has some USD2.4 trillion of foreign exchange reserves of which a large allocation is made to US government bonds and as such has been financing – by its savings – overspending in the US which is 20 times as rich on a per capita GDP basis. Ferguson calls the world with China and America as leading financial powers and this love–hate relationship between them 'Chimerica' (China plus America). So what happens now? China and some other economies which have historically had export-led growth strategies and have run current account surpluses will have to rely more on domestic demand. This should help offset lower domestic demand in economies such as the UK, the US and part of the Eurozone, which have traditionally run large current account deficits. Is this shift feasible? Can the Chinese be turned into a nation of consumers instead of savers? Is it in their culture? What happens if this shift does not take place? Will China's growth falter?

1.7.4 Deleveraging, Slow Job Growth Ahead and Real Estate Bubble Bursts

Firms are still going bankrupt at a high rate, deleveraging is only just starting and unemployment will continue to rise. To use an analogy from Paul Krugman's *The Return of Depression Economics* with a twist, he describes the Asian crisis of the second half of the 1990s and indeed the most recent crisis as '...if bacteria that used to cause deadly plagues...had remerged... even those...who have so far been lucky...would be foolish not to seek new cures...whatever it takes... We were foolish and now the plague is upon us.' In the finale of the Asian crisis, the pain which dragged on as both financial agents and corporates deleveraged was severe, which is indeed the case with the current crisis. The difference is that this time it will be even more painful because the size of the problem is much bigger and leverage levels higher. More importantly, while the Asian crisis impacted other global financial markets, the degree of financial integration at the time was much lower among institutions and markets. Previously, to diversify corporate sources of funding and ease pressure on banking and corporate sectors alike, the crisis 'pressure valve' so to speak, was the development of the local currency bond markets in crisis countries. We do not have this luxury this time round, as the markets that could have acted as a pressure release valve – debt capital markets and derivatives such as CDSs, CDOs or any other CDXXs, have also been deeply affected and our confidence in them deeply shaken. The problem cannot be solved by a 'plain vanilla instrument' or development of markets for them thereof, nor can it be solved by financial innovation which is in part to blame for this crisis. It is no longer the case of 'an emerging market crisis', this is a 'developed market' crisis. As such, the solution will have to be in the form not of an 'antibiotic' as in Professor Krugman's analogy, but a brutal amputation: continued deleveraging.

Businesses will fail and economic activity will suffer as a result, with the 'lemons' (Professor David Akerlof's adverse selection problem in corporate finance theory) resulting in good businesses being punished along with bad businesses. Take for example buying a used car. If you do not know if it is in good condition or one with lots of problems (a lemon), what will be the result? You demand that the seller give you a discount on ALL cars, regardless of whether they are bad lemons or not, because you don't know. This is information asymmetry and the above example an application of the problem to a credit crunch environment.

Business failures will lead to job losses and this will not be helped by the exploding financing problems of developed countries, which will have to cut government spending and in turn more jobs.

1.7.5 So What Happens with Real Estate Now?

Given that a real estate bubble was at the root of this crisis and that real estate affordability indicators in many OECD countries are unfavourable – what will happen now? Are we going to see real estate bounce back as if nothing has happened? How will the weakest sub-sector of real estate, commercial real estate, fare? This current environment *will continue to negatively impact real estate in general and commercial real estate in specific, and in turn result in another round of non-performing loans for banks.*

There are three key indicator sets of house price evolution: house price appreciation year on year, house prices to disposable income ratio and house prices to rent ratio. Using 1992 as the base year with an index value of 100, there are a few OECD countries which have seen drops in house prices in real and nominal terms: Japan, Germany, Switzerland and Korea, the latter saw a drop only in real terms but not in nominal terms. At the other end of the spectrum Ireland for example has seen the largest increase in real estate prices, at 436% in nominal terms and 233% in real terms. There's a clear link here to the real estate-related non-performing loans in Ireland with lending to developers capturing two thirds of GNP, usually without collateral.

Based on this simple index, economies which saw house prices rise by more than 200% very well may have experienced a bubble. These include Australia, the UK, Denmark, New Zealand, Spain, Norway, the Netherlands and Ireland. Not all of these have burst – yet.

1.8 Regulatory Regimes and Response to the Crisis

Hank Paulson's *On the Brink: Inside the Race to Stop the Collapse of the Global Financial System* gives a day-by-day account over a three-month critical period starting September 2008 of what was happening in the US epicentre of the crisis and which regulators did what as both an insider privy to regulation and to investment banking wheeling and dealing from an ex-banker perspective. Hank Paulson served as the 74th secretary of the US Treasury from July 2006 to January 2009 and was both chairman and chief executive of Goldman Sachs. His account shows how all that happened came as a surprise to regulators and how indeed the sheer size of the problem and its implications threw regulators into unchartered territory.

This crisis has triggered much debate as to which regulatory regimes were the most effective: how they dealt with past crises, what actions were taken, the set of policy tools and the impact of these on losses realized and on the speed of crisis unravelling and its resolution. No doubt the ongoing debate in this respect that will shape the face of financial regulation over the coming decades. In academic jargon, preliminary empirical results by Nier (2009) classify the losses associated with each main type of regulatory regime – single-integrated regulator (SIR) versus twin peaks (TP) – in Europe. He finds greater losses associated with the SIR model. The single-integrated regulator model has one regulator overseeing market regulation (commercial banks, mutual funds and pension funds and insurance companies) and the central bank overseeing lender of last resort (LOLR) activities and payments oversight. Examples of SIR-type models are the UK (before June 2010), Denmark, Norway, Sweden and Switzerland among others. TP models have the central bank overseeing systemic risk, including LOLR and payment systems and all potentially systemic institutions and another regulatory body handling regulation of financial services. Examples of TP type systems include the Netherlands, Bulgaria and South Africa, France, Italy, Portugal and Spain. According to Nier (2009), *SIRs have on average lost the equivalent of 3% of total outstanding credit, compared to TP systems, which lost only 0.5%. In terms of value, SIRs collectively lost USD126.4 billion and TPs USD39.6 billion.*

Regulatory policy response to the crisis has been far reaching, from direct intervention in the financial sector through capital injections, purchase of assets, central bank provision of liquidity and guarantees, in addition to traditional coordinated monetary action and fiscal stimulus. Governments have used all the weapons in their artillery to combat the crisis, even applying measures which have not been used in recent history such as quantitative easing. For the latter, the Federal Reserve had announced in March 2009 some USD1.2 trillion for quantitative easing, while the Bank of England had initially announced an outlay of GBP75 billion, which was later raised to GBP175 billion. The measures listed have collectively ranged from less than 1% of GDP to almost 20% in the UK. Central bank balance sheets in the US, the UK and Europe have ballooned, exhibiting growth of around 250%, 220% and a third on the low-end, respectively.

1.9 The Ballooning Fiscal Overhang as a Consequence of Necessary Policy Action

The IMF estimates fiscal stimulus in G-20 countries in 2009 to be around 1.5% of GDP, while overall fiscal balance in advanced economies is projected to deteriorate by 3.25% to −7% percent of GDP in 2009. The US has announced a stimulus package to the tune of 2% of GDP in 2009 and for a total of 4.6% until 2011 (or USD787 billion).

The increase in government debt is forecast to have significant crowding-out effects: for every 10% of increase in government debt, global GDP is forecast to drop by 1.3% (1.2% in the US). Furthermore, fiscal deterioration in advanced economies poses an additional threat to future global growth, as these very same nations have to deal with the effects of a rapidly ageing population and the consequences on pension funding deficits, among others. The first nation to show serious threats to its fiscal position was Greece in October 2009 which has a forecast public debt to GDP for 2010 of 120%, with concerns about the fiscal stability of Portugal (90% of GDP), Spain (68% of GDP) and Italy (130% of GDP). Thus far the IMF has pledged USD1.1 trillion to help developing countries weather the crisis.

1.10 Regulatory Challenges, Proposed Changes and Critique

The IMF identified a set of upcoming policy challenges ahead that will need to be addressed. These include policies to a) secure a backdrop for economic recovery, b) strengthen the banking sector and promote resumption of lending, c) revive securitization markets, d) prevent crises in emerging markets in Europe which remain vulnerable to deleveraging, e) ensure orderly disengagement or exit strategies for regulators, and f) manage the recent transfer of private risks to sovereign balance sheets. It proposes the following priorities for reform: a) restoring market discipline; b) addressing fiscal risks caused by financial institutions (the idea of a 'systemic tax'); c) living wills; d) a macroprudential approach to policy making; e) integrating the oversight of Large and Complex Financial Institutions (LCFIs) into the global financial market. Why is the road map for regulation in the near term so problematic and ultimately challenging?

1.11 Banking Sectors and Individual Institutions are Too Big to: Fail, Regulate, Audit, Manage and Evaluate, in Short Literally Too Big to FRAME

A snapshot of the current size of the banking sectors in a number of countries and indeed the size of selected banks relative to the GDP of their host countries shows an alarming picture, which is again a derivative of the rise in global leverage without which such growth would not have been possible. *Bank assets to GDP range from a high of more than 800% in Switzerland, more than 400% in the UK, to a low of 100% in the US. As banking should finance economic activity, we should expect this ratio to be proportional to the economic activity in a country. Extreme excesses should have raised alarm bells for regulators.* If we look at individual bank balance sheets and turnover, the picture is even more alarming, as per the Goldman Sachs example.

1.12 Selected Proposed Regulatory Changes

The Basle Committee on Banking Supervision (BCBS) and the International Association of Deposit Insurers (IADI) proposed changes to restore the level and quality of bank capital in 2009. These are summarized in the following: a) higher (and better quality) risk-weighted capital requirements, b) countercyclical credit loss provisioning, c) formal leverage ratio, d) mandatory capital insurance or contingent capital, e) convertible capital, f) subordinated debt issuance frequency management, g) prefunding of deposit insurance, and h) capital charges linked to systemic risk.

A number of 'super' or 'uber' regulators were also set up in 2009, including the European Systemic Risk Board (ESRB) to oversee systemic risk at a European level, while in the US these powers were delegated to the Federal Reserve. The mandate of the ESRB is the macroprudential oversight of the financial system within the European Union. The ESRB aims to prevent and mitigate systemic risks within the European financial system in order to prevent financial distress in the European Union. It is also charged with issuing risk warnings, giving recommendations on measures and follow-up on implementation.

1.13 The Way Forward, Macroprudential Analysis and Early Warning Systems for Fragility and Crises

Given the prohibitive cost of crises; output loss estimates of USD10.2 trillion of 'opportunity loss' global GDP and direct write-downs of USD3.4 trillion by agents; and more importantly the *structural* changes that have taken place in the global economy and will unlikely revert to pre-crisis status, the importance of early warning systems for fragility and crises is self-evident. So where do we go from here in terms of macroprudential analysis and early warning systems (EWS) for financial fragility and crises given the failure of pre-existing systems in predicting the current crisis?

First we need to indentify a crisis at a 'pre-crisis' time, namely the build-up of imbalances at the stage of financial fragility using macroprudential analysis tools that cut across markets, sectors and different players both locally and internationally. Analysis of linkages, stress tests and back tests – the whole range of analytical artillery available to supervisors on a national and cross-border level – must be employed, applying further disclosure as the means to bring all these analyses in a timely fashion through enhanced market discipline. If analytical results are required to be disclosed to the market by regulators, this in itself will ensure their timely undertaking and sharing among various national and international players (whether these players are other regulators who also will find this information useful or private sector players, both banks and non-banks, to guide their business strategies).

Second we must find out why EWS which have been in use failed to identify the current crisis and whether this was a system or human failure, or both. EWS have been used historically to a) identify the macro states where policy action is needed (macro-models), b) provide a rating system of individual institutions (micro-models), and c) help policy makers choose the set of tools to use to reduce crises cost. Using a sample of 105 countries, covering the years 1979–2003, Davis & Karim (2008) apply macro EWS models to US and UK data to test for out-of-sample performance (i.e. the performance of a model in the years *after* the time period chosen to build that model. It is a test of model overall relevance in doing what it was designed to do) from 2000–2007. *They find that for the US, both models fail miserably with a probability of a crisis occurring in 2007 using a logit model of only 1% and 0.6% using a binary tree model. For the UK, the results were similar, with logit probability of a crisis at 3.4% in 2007 and 0.6% for the binary tree model.* Clearly, given the crisis has occurred, these models should have shown a high probability of crisis, and therefore failed spectacularly. Alessi and Detken (2009) find that better results for *a set of global liquidity indicators* would have predicted the most recent wave of *asset price booms* (2005–2007), but that the lead time was still too short for policy action.

Third, a global EWS needs to be put in place in line with the recommendations of the De Larosière Report, with all the regulatory implications thereof on a national and cross-border level. This EWS must be guided in design by a meta-theory that takes into account: procyclicality and boundary problems playing on the national and cross-border levels; the trade-off of various regulator objectives; the need for both macroprudential and microprudential analysis and the interaction between them; some degree of built-in countercyclicality as in the Spanish model; and strengthening risk-based supervision by enabling national and cross-border regulators to reduce systemic 'net' risk.

Fourth and most important is that an EWS has to be effective, not just the construct of a large magnitude and political weight. Its effectiveness must be continuously challenged, covering a basic checklist of minimum requirements needed for a robust EWS. These include: pre-crisis sanctions on undercapitalized institutions, that it be *usable* by policy makers and *effective* in identifying stress indicators *with sufficient lead time;* that it is *credible* and *simple enough* to be understood by policy makers at all levels.

We must also understand that each crisis will be different, will have different triggers and will unravel in a different manner to its predecessors. The problem is, as human beings, our perception is always skewed towards what we have seen in our own lifetimes; we do not learn from history and markets do have a short-term memory. In his book *The Black Swan*, Nassim Taleb gives the example of a turkey before Thanksgiving. Every day for 99 days before it is slaughtered, it wakes up, eats, sleeps, wakes up, eats, sleeps, and so on, therefore it is not capable of predicting that it will be killed on the 100th day, because, simply put, this particular turkey has never experienced being slaughtered before, even though many others have before it, and as such it cannot 'perceive' it. We are not programmed to 'see' black swans. As such the best way to prevent a crisis is to ensure that the 'system' is as healthy as possible by attacking imbalances before they accumulate, and recognizing that you cannot predict crises or their timing using a rear-view mirror calibrated model. A model will only help capture imbalance build-up – yes, it is necessary as a starting point, however it is nowhere near sufficient and must be approached as just one of a set of decision packages to be used. The rest is up to human judgement, grounded modesty and ethical action.

1.14 Regulatory Tumbleweed or is it Tangleweed? A Critique of Proposed Changes

In spirit the proposed changes do carry a lot of merit. But the question is why do we need new regulatory bodies and new regulations when working with the pre-existing system and regulations could have helped achieve the results hoped for? I believe this is one of the main hurdles to the effectiveness of regulation, namely focusing on frameworks and power struggles as opposed to what actually gets accomplished on the ground. The Financial Stability Board (FSB) established in 2009 by G-20 leaders, has a predecessor, the Financial Stability Institute (FSI) which was set up in 1999 with a similar mandate. Why did the FSI not sound the warnings for the current crisis? Furthermore, based on empirical research, having SIRs as opposed to TPs for financial agents is precisely what results in information asymmetries.

The banking sector prior to the crisis was highly concentrated, and after the crisis it will be even more so, which brings the concept of too big to **FRAME** to another level. (Banking sector assets to GDP in selected countries and a single bank's assets and turnover to the GDP of a number of nations clearly illustrates this.) Moreover, business cycles are mostly national – what implications does this have on the implementation of countercyclical measures by LCFIs? Does a global regulator promote raising capital requirements when some banking systems in countries which are at the beginning of a credit cycle need to expand to finance growth just because other markets are overheating and are at the end of the credit cycle? And vice versa?

Similarly, criticism of addressing so-called 'crowd pleasers' such as tax havens and bonus structures have been made. Prior to the crisis, irrespective of the level of bonuses, most bank employees actually kept their holdings in the form of shares in their banks. How could caps on payouts as such improve incentives? Why does it matter how much taxes are being 'avoided' by entities operating in tax havens if in the grand scheme of things these taxes 'lost' are very small compared to taxes 'lost' in the case of a business downturn of the financial industry? Shouldn't it be more important to target maximizing net tax receipts in absolute terms? A similar materiality argument holds for bankers' bonuses. I do agree, however, with the need for claw-backs to ensure ethical, non-reckless behaviour.

The global financial regulatory reform agenda is ambitious in its objectives, *however*, an important design element should be how to ensure effectiveness of regulation and remove information asymmetries between same country and cross-border regulators. One way to achieve both would be through greater market discipline, sharing more with participants and players on a national level and *publicly* warning against eminent threats by regulatory bodies. Information shared publicly with the market through preset regular schedules via publications, presentations and hearings at national assemblies should ensure effectiveness. If regulators have to report their performance, then naturally their performance will improve.

One other important design aspect is the governance structures of regulators and protection of whistle-blowers, the more balanced to ensure a diversity of opinions the better. Strengthening the whistle-blower channel means that differing views can and will be heard. Ensuring adequate representation from the private sector on regulatory boards and sufficient 'brainstorming' open discussions with the private sector on upcoming regulations, existing regulations, listening to views from think tanks and independent economists are also crucial to ensure regulators are not 'trapped' in an ivory tower and divorced from the market.

Finally, inclusion of a strong ethical code of conduct and ethics training for both regulators and private sector players is paramount – if anything the last crisis was also a clear crisis of ethics and governance. If mortgage brokers had not extended loans to people who could not repay them, then the subprime market would not have collapsed and the crisis would possibly not have materialized. If mortgage brokers had extended these loans, but we had much lower leverage levels because banks were not seeking extra yield at any cost, the crisis would have been nowhere near what it reached in terms of size. If investment officers were not overzealous in investing in products for which they did not perform sufficient due diligence because they were following the herd, the magnitude of the spillover would have been much less.

In short, if people had better ethics, we would never have crises, period, because excesses will not develop and because if they do, they would be reported and acted upon before it gets too late. Ethics have a quantifiable value, and their value is derived from a complete default scenario. Without ethics, all contractual obligations would not be worth the paper they are written on and indeed markets cannot function. I could use the same argument with every detail pertaining to the crisis discussed in each chapter of this book and indeed the argument could validly be applied to all crises which have occurred in the past, whether they be, financial or otherwise.

Chapter 2

EVOLUTION OF THE STRUCTURE OF THE GLOBAL FINANCIAL SYSTEM PRE-CRISIS AND SYSTEMIC HOT SPOTS

The global financial system changed considerably in the decades preceding the crisis, moving away from plain vanilla instruments, transparent markets and a classical banking model to complex structured products, opaque markets, new banking business models and an exponentially growing shadow banking system. Coupled with a low interest rate environment, this resulted in two main changes in financial player business models: a) a continuous search for yield and more proprietary activities and b) ever-increasing leverage. These changes led to the global financial system becoming 'too big, not only to regulate or to fail, but too big to manage', as coined by leading academic professor Richard Portes. I would like to extend this term further to be too big to FRAME: Too big to Fail, to Regulate, to Audit, to Manage and to Evaluate.

In the Goldman Sachs example, with its revenues in 2007 at USD46 billion of net revenues, of which USD31 billion came from trading and principal investments (68%), we can clearly see the advent of proprietary activities, the yield search and the leverage elements at play. Working some crude numbers to present a simplistic scenario, if we assume Goldman's charged a commission of 1% of notional value of transactions, and all transactions were trading, this would give USD3.1 trillion in dealings by the bank: greater than the GDP of 27 out of the 30 OECD countries in 2007 as noted earlier. There is no doubt these were *highly levered transactions as such*.

A similar picture can be presented for JP Morgan in 2007. JP Morgan booked revenues of USD71.4 billion. Now given its average asset base over 2006 and 2007, this means returns of almost 5% – in a low interest rate environment and a very competitive landscape? How did JP Morgan achieve these results? Again it was playing the leverage game. So what was it doing?

How can any institution of this size be managed? How can it be regulated? How do you deal with its failure?

With low interest rates, and because of an ageing population, liquidity continued to build up and asset price bubbles developed and persisted, both fuelled by excessive leverage. This translated into market underpricing of risk, i.e. underestimating how much risk there really is in the markets and how much return investors would demand for taking on what they perceive as risk. Regulators continued to play catch-up, while roll-out of Basle II, which in theory would have led to better capitalization of the industry in the medium term, resulted in lower capital buffers in the short-term transitional period to full implementation. This chapter focuses on the evolution of the structure of global capital markets before the crisis; the agents and changes in their business models; and finally the development of five key systemic 'hot spots' – namely, weak capitalization, excessive leverage and skewed funding structures of agents, dysfunctional and opaque markets, governance issues and the impact of regulatory changes.

2.1 Capital Markets

A snapshot of the global financial market structure over the past three years shows the notional amount of derivatives as of the end of June 2008 – both exchange traded and over-the-counter (OTC) – registering USD746.9 trillion, of which only USD59.8 trillion was exchange traded and the balance OTC trading opaquely. The notional outstanding amount of derivatives was more than *10 times* global GDP in 2008. By the first half of 2009, OTC derivatives notional fell to USD605 trillion (from USD687.1 trillion), a huge drop of almost USD80 trillion (of which around USD20 trillion is attributed to OTC derivatives which moved to become exchange traded, and the net drop as such is USD60 trillion). Figure 2.1 shows the evolution of the relative size and importance of sub-segments of the global financial markets compared to global GDP. It clearly shows the exponential growth of the derivatives markets, and specifically OTC and the widening gap between GDP growth, which almost looks like a horizontal flat line in comparison. This gap indicates that the boom in derivatives was *pure leverage*. Also the portion of derivatives which was OTC draws a vivid picture of the extent of opacity prevalent.

Figure 2.1 shows how this shock to the system was completely unforeseen by the various market segments ex-ante and that they were only impacted *following* the crisis. This strongly contradicts the efficient market hypothesis (EMH), in its three forms, that all or at least some of all relevant investment information is continually incorporated in markets. The crisis also goes against historical

Figure 2.1. Systemic Hot Spots in Global Market Structure and Market Performance.

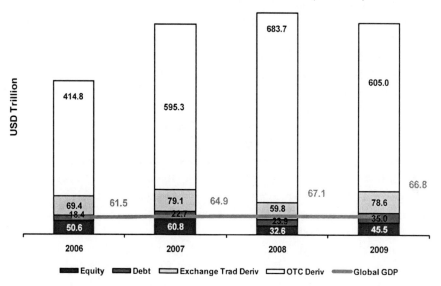

Evolution of Financial Market Structure (2006–09)

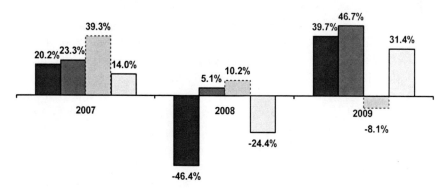

Market Performance in 2007, 2008 and 2009

Sources: World Federation of Stock Exchanges, BIS Quarterly Review (December 2009), IMF.

trends in the data, where equity markets were usually a leading indicator of one to two years of market practitioners' outlook.

What are efficient markets, what is the efficient market hypothesis, and why was this crisis an example of a breach of this hypothesis – so much so that it has led some to claim it has signalled the 'death' of this outdated theory. In simple terms, the efficient market hypothesis states that all information is reflected in market prices of securities. As such one can never hope to beat the market, which more often than not follows a random walk (a term used frequently in the study of finance to indicate that future events cannot be predicted on the basis of past events), because one cannot possibly have information that is not already reflected in prices. There are three forms of EMH. Strong form efficiency is where all public and non-public information about any investment security on the market is already incorporated in the price of this security. The market 'knows it all', the market 'knows best'. At the other extreme is weak form efficiency which states that prices only reflect past publicly available information. Semi-strong efficiency, as the name suggests, lies somewhere in the middle.

Figure 2.1 shows that equity markets actually rose by almost 20% in 2007 and crashed in 2008, falling by 46%. Mapping onto market performance the systemic significance of country equity capital markets in 2008, we can see why the US is the single most systemically significant country in 2008 – capturing 20% of total global equity market capitalization of USD59.8 trillion trailed by Europe with 7%, Japan with 5.2% and the UK with 3%.

In 2009 all global market sub-segments rose significantly – but should this be interpreted as a sign of recovery? Looking at each sub-segment independently, equity capital markets almost recouped their 2008 losses, rising by around 40%. How does this tally with gloomy outlooks for global GDP growth over the coming few years and a bleak macro picture across the board, which in turn implies poor corporate cash flows? My interpretation of this rebound is that analysts have erroneously factored in lower cost of capital, having failed to consider that the shift in risk premiums is permanent and that the current low rate environment will not prevail, with governments sooner rather than later having to raise base rates. Two factors which should raise discount rates plugged into valuation models, each separately. In the case of debt capital markets, the hike in performance is explained for the most part by capital gains resulting from the rapid global drops in interest rates which bolster the value of listed securities. OTC derivatives markets dropped by 8.1%, a sign that this market sub-segment, which is the least transparent, will continue to bleed, while the jump in exchange traded markets is partly explained by the shift in some trading of instruments from OTC markets, as alluded to earlier.

2.1.1 Securitization Market Segment: Special Focus on the US

Securitized instruments, traded both on exchanges and OTC, played a key role in the current crisis because of the way they were employed and the lack of transparency of the underlying claims on which they were based. This despite the fact that securitization as an innovation was initially developed to 'distribute' risk to larger investor groups. By encouraging risk sharing among a larger group of people, the idea was that each investor would end up holding less risk and as such would have more capacity for more activity, thereby promoting growth. Risk is diluted, everyone is better off and the sum of the whole is greater than the parts – perfection is achieved.

Securitization uses however later evolved into many types in addition to genuine credit risk sharing which had a lot of merit, including but not limited to, freeing up risk capital, tapping liquidity niches in capital markets, regulatory arbitrage and credit-risk transfer between agents for asset-liability management (ALM) and/or other risk management purposes. Securitization plays a crucial role in bank wholesale funding and credit extension. There are numerous textbooks on the mechanics and uses of the various types of securitizations which the reader can refer to for a more in-depth review.

So why should something like a seemingly useful financial innovation result in so many problems? One reason is size, the other is details of the structuring – yes the devil still is in the details (Lehman Brother's unwinding is still dragging on in courts why? The small print of the contracts entered into by counterparties which left the terms of settlement and valuation vague in the case of unwinding or worse granted one counterparty more privileges in the case of a loss making contract, in Lehman's case the client, resulting in all clients wanting to exercise these privileges and precipitating Lehman's fall). In terms of size, Figure 2.2 shows that the securitization market is especially important in the US where it captured roughly 28% of outstanding credit in 1Q09 (6% in the Eurozone and 14% in the UK, respectively). The US real estate and consumer credit markets rely heavily on securitization, with government-sponsored enterprises (GSE) and private-label securitizations accounting for 60% of the USD12 trillion outstanding residential mortgage credit, around one quarter of both the USD3.5 trillion commercial mortgages and the USD2.5 trillion consumer credit markets respectively. Thus, these markets commanded a large portion of outstanding credit.

Value investor Warren Buffet dubbed new financial instruments a 'time-bomb' akin to weapons of mass destruction – why? I believe not because of the objectives these instruments were designed to achieve, but rather because of flaws in their design, the how, the (mean) devil hiding in the details – I now turn to look at structuring of these instruments to elaborate on the flaws in their structuring which precipitated this crisis. One important type of instrument

Figure 2.2. Credit Market Structure and Proportion of Securitization.

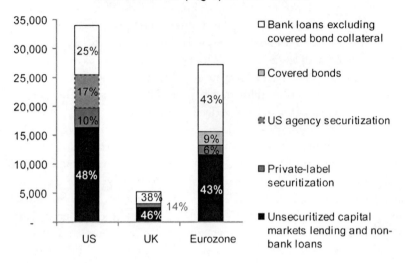

Credit Market Structure: Eurozone, UK and the US (1Q09) in USD Billion

- ☐ Bank loans excluding covered bond collateral
- ▨ Covered bonds
- ✳ US agency securitization
- ▤ Private-label securitization
- ■ Unsecuritized capital markets lending and non-bank loans

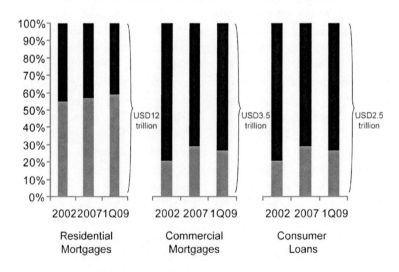

% of Securitization in Select US Credit Classes

▨ Securitized Residential Mortgages ■ Unsecuritized Residential Mortgages

Source: IMF GFSR, October, 2009.

which has received the greatest scrutiny as a key cause of the current crisis is residential mortgage-backed securities, with some critics even going as far as attributing the entire crisis and the ripples which followed to the collapse of this sub-segment, and more specifically to subprime residential mortgage-backed securities. Subprime borrowers by definition are a class of borrowers who normally would not be able to have access to mortgages because of their credit risk profile. Subprime mortgages were designed to allow access to the market by poor quality borrowers, a noble objective, the problem in their design were the terms and self-certification by the borrowers of their own income. These two design flaws made them much more risky and fraught with fraud than would have been the case if they were more ethically and properly managed.

Within this class and across other classes as well, the interest rate terms were either fixed or adjustable. The adjustable rates were extended on the basis of a very low teaser rate interest payment in the first year or two, with the payments rising substantially thereafter. As such, these adjustable rate mortgages (ARMs) had a significant role to play. As long as housing prices continued to rise, buyers refinanced and obtained new mortgages with new teaser rates, thereby avoiding paying the higher rate after the mortgage *resets*. When housing markets collapsed, these buyers were pushed into negative equity and subsequently into default as they could not afford the higher monthly payments. Another design flaw relates to what happened to the mortgage once it had been sold by the mortgage broker. As all end mortgage products were sold to consumers on an originate–distribute basis, mortgage brokers got their commission based on how many mortgages they sold, not on the quality of these mortgages. They then resold these mortgages to banks, who in turn repackaged and sliced and diced them in so many different ways it was impossible for one to tell exactly what the new transformed 'instrument' was. But it didn't matter, because at that point banks simply turned around and sold everything back to the market (distributed the risk), erroneously thinking they were keeping the risk off their books. Neither the rating agencies nor audit firms were able to see this, because the structures and the banks were too big to audit. Thus the originate-and distribute-model effectively reduced the control processes on the granting of these mortgages and also encouraged a high degree of moral hazard.

Michael Moore's *Capitalism* gives a graphic, albeit overly simplistic, view of the crisis, but the statement it makes with regards to how Countrywide for example advertised its products is very relevant to this discussion. Countrywide eventually accepted an emergency loan of USD11 billion from a group of banks to avoid filing for bankruptcy in August 2007.

From Figure 2.2 we can see that the proportion of residential mortgage-backed securities that were private label securitizations (issues structured and/or underwritten by privately owned institutions, not by government-sponsored enterprises) by the end of 2007 stood at around 19%. This is a significant increase from just 8% of the total outstanding volume in 2002. Figure 2.3 also shows this trend by exhibiting the pattern of issuances increasingly shifting to private label issues.

Figure 2.3. European Securitization Markets and ABS Investor Composition.

European Securitization Markets (Euro Billion)

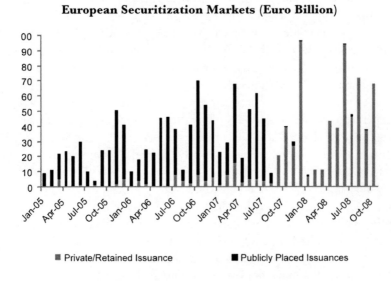

ABS Investor Base Pre-Credit Crunch

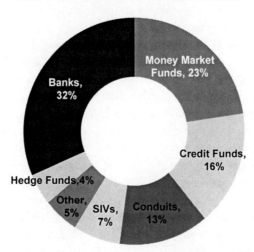

Source: Citi Investment Research, presentation by Simon Samuels, *The Future of Banking*, CFA UK event, 2 December, 2008.

2.1.2 Securitization Market Segment: Europe

In the Eurozone, securitization is less extensively used, with total volume of securitization standing at 6% of total outstanding credit. So how does this explain the paradox of the way in which the collapse of this market segment affected bank balance sheets in Europe? And indeed globally, if pre-crisis banks all over the world bought only a third of all asset-backed security issues as seen in Figure 2.3? According to Citi Investment Research, the majority (72%) of liquidity facilities committed to asset-backed commercial paper (ABCP) globally originated from European banks – thus while European banks were not exposed on the assets side of their balance sheets (indeed they only held a quarter of total outstanding ABCPs in the form of investments in US securitizations), they bore the bulk of the risk of these securities on the liabilities side by providing the liquidity guarantees.

More importantly, these were classified as Triple-A short-term exposures and as such extremely low risk-capital was allocated to this large part of the balance sheet which carried an unforeseen credit and liquidity risk. This helps to explain the magnitude of spillover to European banks through this channel, which is nowhere near proportional to the absolute market size in Europe.

2.2 Agents

After touching upon the structure of the global financial markets in the period before the crisis, the systemic importance of country markets and market sub-segments and the impact of the crisis on these markets, I now turn to discuss the different agents or global financial market players and their key indicators before, during and post the crisis. The abovementioned agents include banks, insurance companies, pension funds, hedge funds and private equity firms, among others. Starting with banks, this section proceeds to talk about insurance companies, other non-bank financial institutions, pension funds, hedge funds, private equity firms, US government-sponsored enterprises (GSE's) and finally special purpose entities (SPEs).

2.2.1 Banks

The global banking industry has changed considerably over the past three years, with banks disappearing and large capital bases being wiped out. In *House of Cards* William Cohan gives an excellent account of what happened in the case of Bear Stearns, which was bailed out on 14 March, 2008 by JP Morgan in conjunction with the Federal Reserve Bank of New York, when the latter agreed to provide an emergency loan to prevent the bank from becoming insolvent. A few days later JP Morgan acquired Bear Stearns, valuing the ailing bank at

$2 a share and bringing back memories of Nick Leeson's role in the collapse of Barings Bank by losing USD1.3 billion on derivatives dealings he undertook in Singapore on the Japanese Osaka exchange. ING went on to acquire Barings Bank for GBP1 in 1995 (one sterling pound for the entire entity and not per share as Barings balance sheet was GBP378 million in negative equity).

And what of the Lehman Brothers? How did it come to file for Chapter 11 bankruptcy in September 2008? In order to understand what happened in the case of individual institutions we must first put in perspective the global banking stage prior to the crisis.

2.2.2 Market Capitalization

The market capitalization of banks in a number of countries gives an indication of their relative systemic significance in a global context. In January 2007, total capitalization of the US banking sector stood at USD1,561 billion, representing 12% of global capitalization. The UK's capitalization stood at USD714 billion (6% of total), the Eurozone (15% of total) and China and Japan each capturing around 5% of global sector capitalization. As of 31 March, 2009, global banking sector capitalization had fallen to almost a third of what it was pre-crisis to USD2.6 trillion. US capitalization stood at USD352.1 billion (14% of total) followed by the UK at USD163.3 billion (6% of total), the Eurozone at USD544 billion (20%), China at USD525.3 billion (20% of total) and Japan at USD249 billion (10% of total). Thus as a result of the crisis, the systemic significance of the US did not decrease: on the contrary it increased; the UK's significance stayed more or less the same as did the Eurozone's significance; however China now suddenly accounts for 20% of the global system and Japan 10%.

2.2.3 Total Assets

According to The Bank for International Settlements (BIS) data, total global banking sector assets (by nationality of ownership of reporting banks) in January 2007 stood at USD29.4 trillion, or 45% of global GDP. This increased to USD39.0 trillion by June 2008, partly as interest rate cuts and mark-to-market valuations of bank balance sheets for a system which is net long, that is with the duration of its assets longer than the duration of its liabilities, inflated balance sheets. In other words, because of the role banks play in terms of maturity transformation in a financial system, a typical bank's balance sheet would consist of long term loans on the assets side and short term deposits on the liabilities side. This means that drops in interest rates would raise the value of loans by much more than it increases the value of deposits, so on a net basis, any bank balance sheet, without the bank itself doing anything, would grown when interest rates decline, and vice versa. As such the drop in interest rates more than offset the portion of asset write-offs and write downs of the total USD3.4 trillion to date, that had taken place over this period. In other words, asset write-downs because of losses, were less than the rise in the 'accounting' rise in valuation of these assets using lower interest rates. By June 2009, and with little support from further rate cuts by policy makers and being hit by larger write-downs, global banking sector assets fell to USD34.1 trillion or 51% of global estimated GDP for 2009. The systemic significance of each country in terms of total assets more or less mirrors that illustrated by market capitalization of its banking sector.

2.2.4 Insurance Companies

In 2007, AIG booked revenues, excluding CDS-related write-offs, of USD30 billion, almost the same figure it booked in 2006. That year CDS-related write-offs amounted to USD11 billion plus. In September of 2008 AIG was bailed out by the US government for a total of USD85 billion; in exchange the US Federal Reserve Bank got stock warrants for 79.9% of AIG equity. To be able to comprehend this turn of events we must again put the structure of this industry into perspective.

An attempt to map the structure of the global insurance industry in terms of market share based on direct gross premiums indicates the US captured a hefty 36% as of end of 2007, the UK 14%, Japan 9% and the Eurozone 21%, respectively. Layering on top of market shares, information on insurance premiums as a percentage of GDP shows an 11% share in the US, almost 20% in the UK, Japan 7% and for the Eurozone (excluding Ireland) 7% on average, respectively in 2007. This clearly indicates the importance of the US insurance market in the global insurance industry.

In terms of industry-risk profiles, Figure 2.4 shows the breakdown between life and non-life within each country, alluding to its risk profile (as non-life is riskier), with shorter, front-loaded pay-off structures than life. The US industry is composed of around 60% non-life, its gross insurance premiums comprise 11% of US GDP and its insurance industry is a third of the global insurance market in terms of premium market share, highlighting the *systemic significance* of any shocks to the US insurance market. In the UK, 22% of the insurance industry is non-life and gross insurance premiums are almost 20% of GDP, while the UK insurance industry represents around a sixth of the global insurance market. This shows the UK's global systemic significance, ranking second after the US, but with a less risky profile. Japan's non-life portion of the insurance industry is around 22%, while the Eurozone's is 50% on average

Figure 2.4. Insurance Market Shares and Product Segmentation.

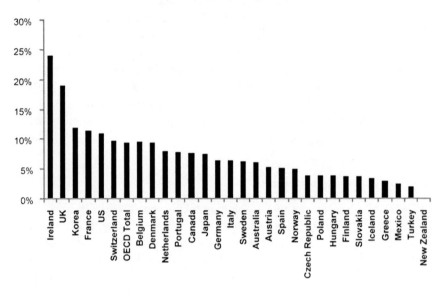

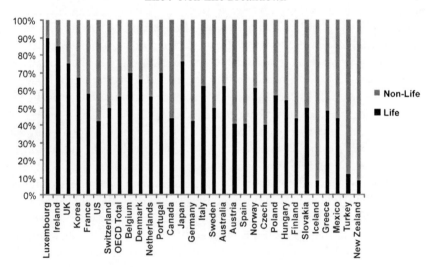

Source: *OECD Insurance Statistics Yearbook*, 1998–2007, 2009 edition.

(excluding Ireland). This mapping gives a rough picture of the risk of the industry in each country and its contribution to global risk.

2.2.5 Insurance Companies and Securitization

Other than being investors in asset-backed securities themselves – for which the extent of their exposure thereof was capped by strict investment guidelines requiring high diversification of holdings – insurance companies were directly exposed to securitization markets through guarantees provided to 'enhance' an issue's credit rating to Triple-A.

AIG claims to have stopped providing credit enhancement for subprime mortgage issues in 2005, according to Bloomberg, but is this really true? In essence they continued to provide credit enhancement in other forms, using other instruments (such as CDSs which explains the write-down in 2007).

Another sub-segment of the insurance market is made up of 'mono-line insurers' that specialize in financial guarantees. Eleven of these firms, which included MBIA, Ambac, CIFG, and ACA Financial Guaranty (all poorly capitalized), guaranteed more than *USD2.4 trillion* of asset-backed securities. These companies banked on their own Triple-A ratings to provide guarantees and, according to Bloomberg estimates early on in the crisis, would have resulted in some USD200 billion in securities losses to the securities they guaranteed had they been downgraded themselves. As the crisis unravelled in the subsequent months, these insurers did indeed lose their Triple-A status, followed by full-fledged downgrades to sub-investment status and in turn the issues they guaranteed were also affected. The latest was Ambac's downgrade in the 3Q09 to junk status, CC− by S&P and MBIA to BB+. Given that Ambac is almost half the size of MBIA, the difference in ratings downgrades is understandable as Ambac's capitalization was much smaller than MBIA's.

2.2.6 Other Non-Bank Financial Institutions

As of early 2007, near-bank entities globally had an estimated **USD15 trillion** in assets (standing at almost half traditional global banking sector assets). One of the largest non-bank financial institutions, GE Capital, had assets of around USD0.6 trillion, slightly less than Morgan Stanley's and larger than US Bancorp and Bank of New York Mellon. On 12 March, 2009, Standard & Poor's (S&P) downgraded GE Capital's long-term ratings from AAA to AA+, with only five non-bank financials (down from 50 in 1980) continuing to have a triple-A rating from S&P as of this date.

GMAC, the former finance arm of General Motors, which had around a third of its assets allocated to mortgage finance through Residential Capital, known as ResCap, was bailed out by the US government over the course of 2009 with injections of more than USD16 billion. Little information is available on other non-bank financial institutions and their financial strength.

2.2.7 Pension Funds

The world faces an increase in longevity and a rising number of pensioners that in its own right poses a serious threat to developed countries' fiscal standing. The developed world is ageing, and increasing the retirement age, as the UK did recently, is but a sedative that will not solve the real problem of underfunded pension schemes. This not only results in the need for pension yields to rise to help counter an expanding pension fund deficit, but also highlights the need to safeguard existing pension assets.

Total pension assets in 46 countries surveyed by the OECD stood in excess of *USD25 trillion* at the end of 2007. Sixteen of these have pension fund investments in equities and mutual funds greater than 10% of GDP. These include Australia, the US, Canada, Iceland, the Netherlands, Switzerland, Denmark and the UK, while emerging markets with high exposures include South Africa, Chile and Brazil. During 2008 estimated losses of pension funds due to market turmoil in the US were 22% of GDP (USD3.2 trillion) and 31% (USD0.7 trillion) in the UK. The OECD estimates that around 3% (USD0.75 trillion) of total pension fund assets surveyed are exposed to potentially toxic assets. Furthermore, increases in risk aversion by investors, *ceteris parabis*, would also lead to a drop in asset values. A research note by Morgan Stanley highlights the impact of an increase in investor risk aversion based on an in-house designed index and an extensive investor survey, this is graphically presented in Figure 2.5 (below).

2.2.8 Longevity Risk, Hedging and the Search for Yield

Pension funds know that they are facing huge longevity risks, this is a large push for the reckless search for yield and investments into asset classes which are little understood. As pension funds are providers of long-term liquidity in capital markets, in the past crisis, providing this liquidity to invest in securitized instruments helped in the growth of these markets. In the UK for example, each additional year beyond the age of 65 pensioners live is estimated to cost GBP30 billion, adding 3% to pension liabilities.

This brings us to a discussion of longevity risk as an important source of risk when we talk about pension funds. Longevity risk is the risk that there will be unanticipated increases in life expectancy and as such organizations which supply annuities will find themselves having to provide them for longer.

Figure 2.5. Pension Fund Assets Evolution in OECD (1995–2007)* and Impact of Risk Aversion on Asset Values.**

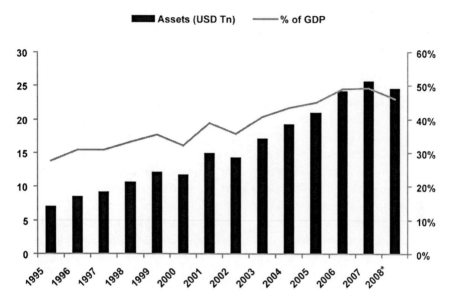

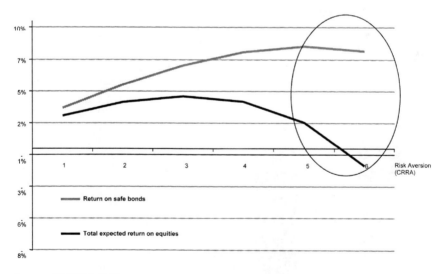

Sources: OECD & IMF.
*estimate. **Includes private and public pension plan assets. **Morgan Stanley Research, Professor David Miles.

According to *CFA Magazine*'s April 2010 issue and a World Economic Forum (WEF) report on longevity risk, pension debts have devastated General Motors, stopped the New York City subways and led to the bankruptcy of the city of San Diego and could very well bear the seeds of the next financial crisis.

2.2.9 Hedge Funds

The USD2.0 trillion hedge fund industry has been under significant stress since the beginning of the crisis on the back of high asset-weighted leverage ranging from 10x to 17x. Figure 2.6 shows the breakdown of funds that failed, their total assets and asset-weighted leverage. A total of 62 funds with different specializations have failed over the period from June 2007 to August 2008. Examples include hedge fund Basis Yield Alpha, run by Australia's Basis Capital, with a capitalization of USD700 million at the beginning of 2007, which turned insolvent when its holdings of CDOs crashed in value in the summer and it could not face margin calls from lending banks which demanded extra

Figure 2.6. Large Hedge Fund Failures on the Back of the Crisis.

Strategy	No.	Assets[1]	Asset-Weighted Leverage[2]
Fixed-Income	31	97	16
Structured Products	21	79	17
Sovereign/Macro	4	8	14
Other fixed income	6	10	10

[1]USD billion. [2]Leverage defined as the ratio of assets to equity capital

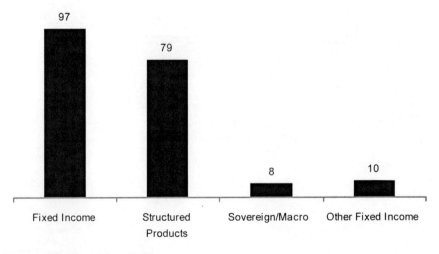

Source: Bloomberg LP and IMF.

collateral. Another example is Drake Management flagship USD3.0 billion macro hedge fund, one of the best performing funds in 2006 that yielded an annual return of 41%. Drake Management requested a voluntary freeze on fund withdrawals from its investors and the fund fell 10% in October 2007 and 14% in November 2007 on the back of bets against US treasuries.

2.2.10 Private Equity Firms

According to PSEPS, the largest open private equity and venture capital directory, the estimated capitalization of the world's top 100 funds stood at around USD418.4 billion (this estimate is based on different reporting years, and as such should be treated as a general indicator of systemic significance rather than a real-time industry statistic). This industry's business model is highly dependent on leverage for its return structure, with the proportion of equity in recent transactions getting smaller and smaller, and exit returns mainly capitalizing on a high leverage multiplier, *as opposed to significant real value creation in investees*. As such the recent crisis will have a long-term impact on these agents, as the banking sector shuns higher risk deals and faces a continued credit crunch as it deleverages towards pre-crisis levels. Exiting from investments will also become difficult, as financing dries out and stock flotations of buyouts (which usually are younger, riskier firms) having less appeal in a heightened risk-averse environment.

If we take private equity activity in the UK as an example, investment in buyouts in the UK in the first half of 2009 booked GBP3.2 billion, according to the latest data from the Centre for Management Buyout Research (CMBOR) of the University of Nottingham. This is down from GBP12.5 billion in the same period last year and is the lowest half-yearly figure since 1995. In terms of deals by value, the number of deals and the value of deals have fallen considerably. Deals below GBP10 million reached just GBP206 million by value and 126 in number. The lower-mid market, which is defined as deals between GBP10 million and 100 million, has been mostly affected, with just 14 deals in H1 2009, whilst there have only been five deals above GBP100 million after 39 in 2008 and 67 in 2007.

The picture in Europe is similar, total value slumped to 10.3 billion euros for the first half of 2009 – far lower than the value for the same period in the previous year (42.4 billion euros). The total number of deals was 384 in total, much fewer than the same period in 2008 (705).

2.2.11 US Government-Sponsored Institutions (GSEs)

The systemic significance of Fannie Mae and Freddie Mac is huge. Fannie and Freddie were originally created to help ensure that financing for homes would be available and affordable to more consumers. The two firms buy mortgages from banks and other lenders and bundle them together into securities. They then either hold those securities or sell them to investors with a guarantee that they will be paid the money owed by homeowners. Collectively they held around USD5.3 trillion of mortgage-related exposure (USD3.7 trillion in mortgages securitized and USD1.6 trillion held directly in their portfolios). GSEs debt also comprises approximately one quarter of the USD31 trillion of total outstanding US bond market debt. As such the federal government organized a takeover of Fannie Mae and Freddie Mac in September 2008. The combined losses of both institutions amounted to USD14.9 billion and the Treasury committed to invest as much as USD200 billion in preferred stock and extend required credit through 2009 to keep both institutions afloat. By the end of 2009 Fannie Mae had received more than USD34 billion and Freddie Mac more than USD51 billion.

2.2.12 Special-Purpose Entities (SPEs)

The BIS issued a comprehensive report on Special Purpose Entities (SPEs) in September 2009, highlighting the nature of the various vehicles, motivation for their use, impact on risk disintermediation and the degree of risk transfer, accounting implications and regulatory capital implications. One particular type of SPE, Special Investment Vehicles (SIVs), was prominent in the past crisis. Unregulated and off-balance sheet, this was a vehicle for banks to raise cheap liquidity to fund long-term investments and profit from the spread differential in a low-interest rate environment. Relying on the wholesale short-term funding market, however, and undertaking a huge tenor mismatch and also disguised credit risk by investing in pseudo 'Triple-A', 'high-yield' securities was a recipe for disaster. When funding dried up, these off-balance sheet entities drew on the contingent credit lines of their sponsors and in effect transformed into on-balance sheet entities for the sponsors, not because of contractual obligations but because of reputational concerns by their sponsors. According to Turner (2009), total assets held in the form of SIVs amounted to USD300 billion in 2007, of which less than USD50 billion was equity financed. A list of SIVs and their main sponsors is provided in Figure 2.7.

Given that the portion of equity financing was minimal, rollover of short-term funding was key to the survival of these vehicles. Bloomberg research showed that outstanding MTN for the existing SIVs as of December 2007 stood at around USD181 billion, which is a sizable portion of the total USD300 billion estimated size of SIVs. Research by Dresdner bank showed that around USD40 billion was to be repaid from January to March 2008 alone, and the following MTN were to be repaid by SIVs before September 2008: Sigma Finance (USD22.5 billion), Cullinan Finance (USD19.0 billion), DrK (USD13.4 billion) and Citigroup (USD29.1 billion).

Figure 2.7. SIVs and their Sponsors in 2007.

No.	SIV	Sponsor	No.	SIV	Sponsor
	Bank Sponsored			Bank Sponsored	
1	Nightingale Finance	AIG	17	Hudson-Thames Capital	MBIA
2	Carrera Capital Finance	NSH Nordbank	18	Premier Asset Collateralized Entity (PACE)	SG
3	Parkland Finance	Bank of Montreal	19	Whistle Jacket Capital	Standard Chartered Bank
4	Links Finance	Citigroup	20	White Pine Corp	Standard Chartered Bank
5	Beta Finance	Citigroup	21	Harrier Finance	WestLB
6	Centauri Corporation	Citigroup		Independent Sponsors	
7	Dorada Finance	Citigroup	22	Axon SIV	Axon Financial
8	Five Finnce Corp	Citigroup	23	Kestrel Funding	Brightwater Capital
9	Sedna Finance	Citigroup	24	Cheyne Finance	Cheyne Capital
10	Vetra Finance	Citigroup	25	EV Variable Leveraged Fund	Eaton Vance
11	Zela Finance	Citigroup	26	Orion Finance	Eiger Capital
12	Tango Finance	Citigroup & Rabobank	27	Sigma Finance	Gordian Knot
13	K2 Corporation	Dresdner Kelinwort	28	Theta Finance	Gordian Knot
14	Asscher Finance	HSBC	29	Abacus Investments	III Offshore Advisors
15	Cullinan Finance	HSBC	30	Cortland Capital	IXIS/Ontario Teachers
16	Rhinebridge	IKB	31	Victoria Finance	Ceres Capital Partners

Source: Newspapers and Wikipedia, June and December, 2007.

2.3 Systemic Hot Spots

From the preceding two sections a number of issues crystallize as intuitive systemic hot spots which developed before the crisis and set the conditions for the subsequent meltdown:

i) the size of the global derivatives market and the proportion of OTC activity in this market in comparison to global GDP were huge, the OTC market was 10x global GDP in 2008 – thus the global macro system on the whole was highly leveraged. Only a fraction less than 10% of derivatives was exchange traded, and the balance of OTC trading was opaque with no centralized clearing house.

ii) securitization, while in itself a worthy tool for credit-risk transfer and management, failed miserably in achieving any of its stated objectives and resulted in excessive leverage on the micro level for individual agents and skewed funding structures in terms of investor base and tenors.

iii) the US was systemically the most significant single country in terms of its *market share* and *structural composition* of:
   a. its capital markets which constituted a fifth of the world's capitalization (with almost one third of its credit market sub-segment in the form of securitized issues),
   b. its banking sector (12% of the global system capitalization and with its largest number of affiliated SIVs),
   c. insurance companies premium global market share of 36% and the percentage of non-life activities within the sector in the US,
   d. hence, in hindsight, the global system was especially vulnerable to any shocks in the US.

iv) Roll-out of Basle II and the partial implementation both in terms of institutions and of the full scope of the new accord.

v) Governance and ethical issues, specifically related to the US subprime mortgage (NINJA loans, LIAR loans, etc.), a key factor in the ratchet of defaults, mainly of adjustable-rate mortgages, which tipped the balance of the entire system given the above preconditions, and more generally related to the originate-and-distribute model, resulting in no effective risk transfer taking place; and

vi) the simultaneous occurrence of all these factors together, given the previous conditions resulted in a total meltdown of the global system and the need for rethinking global regulatory regimes. The following section discusses each hot spot in more detail.

2.3.1 Weak Capitalization, Excessive Leverage and Skewed Funding Structures

Weak capitalization and excessive leverage are major culprits in increasing bank fragility. This links back to our discussion about changing banking business models, the Goldman Sachs and JP Morgan examples given earlier.

A decomposition analysis of US, Euro and UK banks return on equity, using on-balance sheet data sourced from Bankscope in 1996 and 2007, shows that the increase in banking sector return on equity (RoE) over the period was predominantly a pure leverage play, where ROE = return on assets (RoA) x leverage. Had this increase in leverage not taken place, due to increased competition and smaller spreads, banking return on assets would have been much lower. This is especially true for the UK, which saw leverage increase from 18x in 1996 to 28x in 2007. Figure 2.8 shows the decomposition of RoE for US, UK and European banks on the left.

Note that the data for the US shows reduced leverage, this could be partially explained by the shift to off-balance sheet financing and the growth of securitization as a proportion of the US credit market.

As leverage normalizes to pre-crisis levels, and if we assume pre-crisis levels to be 25x, as shown in the right panel of Figure 2.8, we would see normalized post-crisis RoEs of around 14% across Europe, 12.1% for the US and 16.6% for the UK. If we assume more aggressive deleveraging to only 10x, RoEs would fall to 6.6% in the US, 5.4% in Europe and 4.8% in the UK. This is proof that the shift in the banking industry is a structural one, with real impact on business models, and *not* a transitory shock after which we will return to pre-crisis norms. Moreover this simulation does not take into account increased regulatory burdens, whether they are in the form of 'systemic taxes' or others. With lower profitability, it will take longer to build capital buffers.

2.3.2 Skewed Funding Structures: The 'Composition' of Leverage also Matters

The funding structure of banks over the same period reflects some core shifts, while deposits and short-term funding continue to constitute a stable percentage of around two thirds of total balance sheet funding. The *proportion of wholesale funding as a percentage of total deposits and short-term funding shows a massive shift*, rising from 24% in the US in 1996 to 40% in 2007, from 7% in Europe in 1996 to 19% in 2007 and from 29% in the UK in 1997, to a whopping 84% in 2007. The shifts in funding structures in various countries are shown in Figure 2.9. On the left, the percentage money market funding/total deposits and short-term funding is presented, while the right panel shows the aggregate shift for US, UK and European banks.

The reliance on wholesale funding markets as such resulted in increased vulnerability to liquidity shocks, which was exactly what took place in the last crisis. Furthermore, because of the higher portion of short-term funding in banks' total sources of funding, the impact on funding cost will be huge as

Figure 2.8. RoE Decomposition 1996 vs 2007 Proforma RoEs for Various Leverage Scenarios.

	1996	2007
ROA		
US Banks	1.2%	0.7%
UK Banks	0.8%	0.5%
Europe	0.5%	0.5%
Leverage		
US Banks	15.4	14.7
UK Banks	18.2	27.7
Europe	25.9	38.6
RoE		
US Banks	18.1%	9.8%
UK Banks	15.2%	13.4%
Europe	14.0%	20.8%

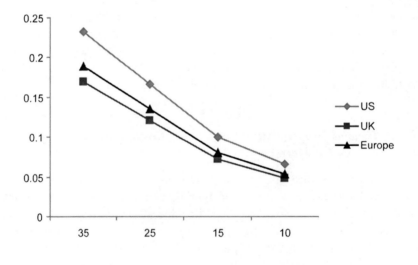

Leverage (x)	35	25	15	10
US	23.3%	16.6%	10.0%	6.6%
UK	16.9%	12.1%	7.2%	4.8%
Europe	18.9%	13.5%	8.1%	5.4%

Source: Author's calculations, data from Bankscope.
*Europe excluding UK, data from Citi Investment Research.
**RoE = RoA x Leverage.
***Leverage = Assets/Equity.

Figure 2.9. Increased Reliance on Money Market Funding (1996 vs 2007).

% Money Market Funding/T. Deposits & ST Funding

	1996	2007
Austria	20%	12%
Belgium	0%	17%
Denmark	0%	7%
Finland	18%	43%
France	12%	39%
Germany	1%	31%
Greece	1%	5%
Iceland	0%	17%
Ireland	3%	34%
Italy	7%	11%
Luxembourg	3%	5%
Netherlands	2%	24%
Norway	7%	5%
Portugal	1%	9%
Spain	20%	27%
Sweden	14%	23%
Switzerland	5%	28%
Turkey	8%	6%
Average	**7%**	**19%**

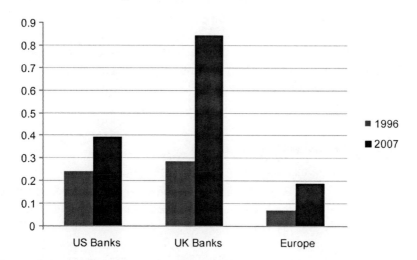

Source: Author's calculations, data from Bankscope.

soon as interest rates start rising again. It is also likely that funding costs are going to remain higher on the back of lower proportion of cheap wholesale funding and the shift in risk premiums.

2.3.3 Dysfunctional and Opaque Markets

Commonly cited causes of the crisis are failure of the originate and distribute model or the design of subprime mortgages, the growth and lack of quality mortgages due to securitization and rating agencies' rubber-stamping of Triple-A ratings on the basis of credit enhancements provided mostly by poorly capitalized mono-line insurers. According to Acharya-Richardson (2009), the core factor was in fact the lack of credit transfer. While in theory bank sponsors of asset-backed commercial paper conduits (ABCPs) and SIVs were vehicles for credit-risk transfer – taking credit risk off the balance sheets and 'distributing' it at large to the market, thereby freeing risk capital and transforming their sponsors risk profiles – in reality, no credit-risk transfer took place outside the financial sector. This is clearly illustrated by Figure 2.10, which shows that banks ended up holding USD4.2 trillion in instruments linked to the housing market on the assets side of their balance sheets as loans and investments – 40% of the total market. Government-sponsored organizations – GSEs and the Federal Home Loan Banks (FHLB) – held 14% of the market and other financial players held the balance.

Sponsors invested heavily in each other's vehicles (40% of the risk stayed with the banking sector on the investment side) while banks had also guaranteed on average 95.7% of USD1.2 trillion ABCP assets for which they were sponsors but had classified as 'off-balance' sheet – and were therefore unregulated and *opaque*. The ten largest ABCP issuers had ratios of ABCP assets to equity as high as 336% for WestLB, 201% for ABN Amro and 106% for HBOS as illustrated by the top right of Figure 2.11. Thus, total banking sector undercapitalization on the back of 'off-balance' sheet activity pre-crisis was at least to the tune of USD64.1 billion as shown by the left panel of Figure 2.11.

2.3.4 Governance Issues and Ethics

Barrell (2008) identifies three key features of the development of the last crisis which are related to governance in the financial sector: a) lending standards had become too lax in many countries, with loan-to-value ratios of 125% in the UK and the US, 2) bank lending grew exponentially and loan defaults rose, iii) products became complex and reliance on rating agencies extensive and less regulated. These are just a few. Other governance issues

Figure 2.10. No Credit-Risk Transfer.

	Loans	HELOC	Agency MBS	Non-Agency Triple-A	CDO Subordinated	Non-CDO Subordinated	Total	%
Bank & Thrifts	2,020	869	852	383	90		4,214	40%
GSEs & FHLB	444		741	308			1,493	14%
Brokers/dealers			49	100	130	24	303	3%
Financial Guarantors		62			100		162	2%
Insurance Companies			856	125	65	24	1,070	10%
Overseas			689	413	45	24	1,171	11%
Other	461	185	1,175	307	46	49	2,223	21%
Total	2,925	1,116	4,362	1,636	476	121	10,636	100%
%	28%	10%	41%	15%	4%	1%	100%	

Source: Viral V. Acharya, Presentation on 'Restoring Financial Stability, How to Repair a Failed System', CFA event, 1 June 2009.

Figure 2.11. Capital 'Shortfall' is Large for Some Banks, No Regulatory Capital Kept for 'Off-Balance Sheet'.

USD Billion

Name	Equity	ABCP	Missing Capital	%
Citigroup	90.9	92.7	6.7	7.4%
ABN Amro	31.2	68.6	5.5	17.6%
Bank of America	91.1	45.7	3.7	4.1%
HBOS	44	43.9	3.5	8.0%
JP Morgan	81.1	42.7	3.4	4.2%
HSBC	87.8	39.4	3.2	3.6%
Deutsche	31	38.7	3.1	10.0%
Societe Generale	34.1	38.6	3.1	9.1%
Barclays	45.2	33.1	2.6	5.8%
Rabobank	34.8	30.8	2.5	7.2%
WestLB	9.5	29.9	2.4	25.3%
ING	42	26.4	2.1	5.0%
Mitsubishi	63.9	26	2.1	3.3%
Dresdner Bank	16.4	23.2	1.9	11.6%
Fortis	21.9	22.6	1.8	8.2%
Bayerische Landesbank	14.1	22.4	1.8	12.8%
State Street Corp	6.5	21.9	1.6	24.6%
Credit Agricole	39.5	19.5	1.6	4.1%
Hypo Real Estate	6.1	18.9	1.5	24.6%
Lloyds TSB	25.2	18.8	1.5	6.0%
RBS	52.3	15.8	1.3	2.5%
Royal Bank of Canada	19.1	15.6	1.2	6.3%
KBC Group	17.6	12.6	1	5.7%
Sachsen Bank	1	12.5	1	100.0%
BNP Paribas	55.6	11.6	0.9	1.6%
Bank of Montreal	14.8	11.5	0.9	6.1%
Wachovia	39.4	10.8	0.9	2.3%
Sumitomo	39.6	9.6	0.8	2.0%
Landesbank Baden-Wuerttemberg	14.1	8.4	0.7	5.0%
Total	**1,070**	**812.2**	**64.3**	**6.0%**

(*Continued*)

Figure 2.11. Continued.

Ten Largest ABCP Conduit Sponsors

USD Billion	ABCP	Assets	Equity	ABCP/Equity
Citibank	93	1,884	120	77.5%
ABN Amro	69	1,301	34	202.9%
Bank of America	46	1,464	136	33.8%
HBOS	44	1,160	42	104.8%
JPMorgan Chase	42	1,352	116	36.2%
HSBC	39	1,861	123	31.7%
Societe Generale	39	1,260	44	88.6%
Deutsche Bank	38	1,483	44	86.4%
Barclays	33	1,957	54	61.1%
WestLB	30	376	9	333.3%

Banks Had to Take Back Assets

USD Billion	ABCP	% Assets Returned to Banks
Full Liquidity	752	100%
Full Credit	160	100%
Extendible Notes	227	92.3%
SIVs	93	73.8%
All Conduits	1,232	95.7%

Source: Viral V. Acharya, 'Presentation on Restoring Financial Stability, How to Repair a Failed System', CFA event, 1 June 2009.

cited after the crisis include accounting firms approving bank financials with no qualifications (Icelandic bank auditor's offices were recently raided for evidence); bonus structures skewed to front-end gains, with insufficient claw-back provisions; weak and poorly represented risk management functions; lack of proper whistleblower channels and structure and composition of bank boards. These in themselves are symptoms rather than causes of weaker moral fibre and ethics. Even in the absence of governance structures, strong ethical frameworks, codes of conduct or whatever label attached to the latter, would have helped partially prevent or minimize losses from the past crisis. This underscores the importance of ethical conduct and ethics enhancement in an individual and institutional setting.

2.3.5 Regulatory Changes

BIS is the central bank for bankers. Established in 1930 and headquartered in Basle in Switzerland, the BIS oversees the regulation of the global banking industry. In 1988, the first Basle Accord was ratified regulating minimum capitalization and risk measurement practices for the global industry. In 2004 the second Basle Accord, Basle II, with its more risk-sensitive approach, was rolled out for adoption by global banks and was expected to have been adopted universally by 2010. Could the adoption of Basle II have caused the crisis as some academics and practitioners claim?

It is unlikely, although it did cause systemically important institutions with established risk management departments and IT systems to end up with lower capital buffers because they qualified for the use of internal ratings-based approaches and presented stress test results to regulators using sophisticated models, which the latter were still in the process of evaluating in terms of robustness and assumptions. The remaining smaller banks and markets were running to catch up with the pack but had not yet implemented the accord.

In concept, Basle II was not to blame – had the implementation been fully carried through, it would have been robust enough to warrant the higher capital buffers required. The three pillars of the accord are sufficiently comprehensive and all-encompassing to ensure that, with the supervisory and market discipline pillars complementing the amended Basle I, Basle II is a truly risk-sensitive dynamic framework and a significant improvement over the static Basle I. Going back to rely solely on fixed capital rules and leverage ratios, while underscoring sensibility and common sense, is not necessarily the best route. Perhaps implementing the modified Basle II accord to take into account liquidity risks, reinstate some static common sense metrics, improve stress testing mechanisms within the supervisory pillar and significantly strengthen the market discipline pillar could be the answer.

Chapter 3

CRISIS UNRAVELLING
AND KEY EVENTS

'Greed, ladies and gentlemen, for lack of a better word is *good*,' says Gordon Gecko, played by Michael Douglas, in the 1987 movie *Wall Street*. Then, when lecturing his protégé trader in the movie *Bud Fox* (played by Charlie Sheen), he claims, 'I create nothing, I *own*...we create the rules'.

Before the crisis had gathered full speed, then-senator Barack Obama, in a speech to Wall Street ('A Call to Conscience' on 17 September 2007) postulated that it could not be right for a few to reap the fruits of a nation, to justify outsized paydays on Wall Street as part of the natural order of things and that Americans have to remind themselves that, 'We rise and fall as one nation'. Was Obama able to predict the fiscal cost from bailouts that ensued and that indeed the burden would be borne by the general public, the taxpayers? Can the crisis build-up and unravelling be simplistically framed as such? Not really. Vilifying bankers and financial sector players is not constructive if we want to absorb lessons from this crisis to avoid future ones rather than over focusing on who was to blame, which is not useful. However, there were elements of greed, of the financial sector 'creating' nothing in physical terms and of unjustified paydays. Can the crisis be framed in light of Warren Buffet's March 2003 claim that derivatives are 'financial weapons of mass destruction' and a time-bomb waiting to explode? Again there is an element of truth to this, but only within the context of how derivatives as a 'tool' were used.

Imbalances were building in the US economy fuelled by low interest rates, exacerbated by the behavioural elements above. As the US housing market turned, a segment of the subprime securitized mortgage loans with adjustable rates started to default, leading to the bankruptcy of two mortgage lenders Ownit Mortgage Solutions at the end of 2006, followed by New Century Financial in April 2007. This was followed by the collapse in June 2007 of two highly leveraged Bear Stearns hedge funds. Acharya (2009) points to the two underlying factors being at play: an *asset price bubble* and a *credit boom*. What started as credit losses in one market sub-segment spilled over into a confidence crisis, shifting of risk premiums and in turn almost complete drying-up of liquidity

Figure 3.1. The Evolutionary Development of the Crisis of 2007–10.

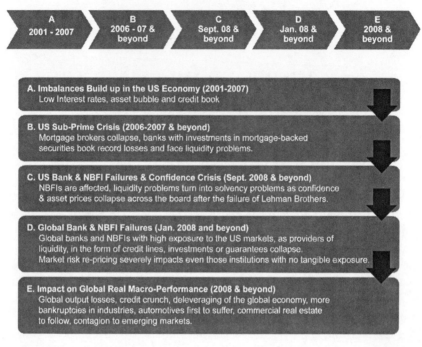

Source: Author's depiction.

and wholesale funding markets. This spiralled into self-fulfilling prophecies of asset sales to meet margin calls leading to more asset sales and value collapsed across all markets. Figure 3.1 presents the evolution of the crisis in a number of *overlapping* phases and key turning points from A. US Local Imbalances; to B. The US Subprime Crisis; to C. US & NBFI Failures & Confidence Crisis; to D. Global Bank & NBFI Failures; to E. Impact on Real Macro Performance: The Evolutionary Development of the Crisis. A detailed time-log of crisis events across the globe is presented in Appendix 1, while Appendix 2 presents: A Brief History of Crises Episodes in the Past.

The following sections discuss each phase separately.

3.1 Imbalance Build-Up in the US Economy (2001–07)

On the back of a low interest rate environment, with Federal Funds rates remaining at 1% between June 2001–04, two main imbalances developed in the US economy. These were an asset price bubble and a leverage build-up or credit boom. The former manifested itself in rising housing prices and stock market and commodities appreciation, while the latter impacted overall levels of indebtedness of the economy and households. According to the OECD, over the period from 1996 to 2006, the ratio of house prices to household income in the US increased from 87% to more than 110%. Looking at an index which combines the S&P, NASDAQ, gold, real estate, the 10-year treasury note and the US dollar – the All-the-Same-Market Composite Index

Figure 3.2. OECD Home Price-to-Income Ratios and Household Indebtedness Relative to Disposable Income.

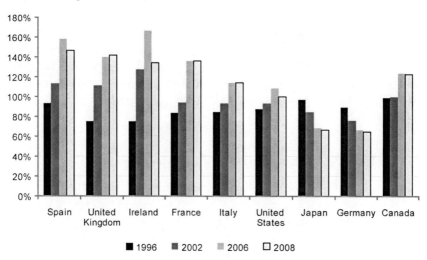

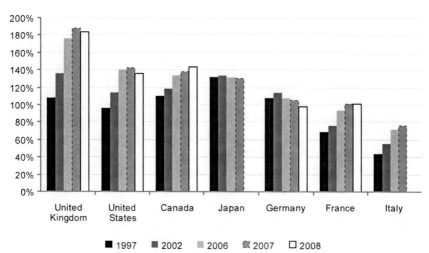

Price to income ratio is defined as the ratio of nominal house prices to per capita disposable income compared to a long-term average calibrated to 100 using an econometric model. Household Indebtedness to Disposable Income is defined as total household credit to disposable income. Source: OECD.

(ASMI), a proxy for appreciation of all asset classes with 1997 as a base year set at 100, shows the index peaking at more than 200 on 3 July, 2008. Trailing price-earnings ratio for stocks listed on the NYSE was 46 times, this compares to 31 times in 1999 during the dot com bubble and 42 times in 2003. A price-earnings ratio of 46 times means that investors will have to wait 46 years to recoup their investment in a stock today. At the same time, levels of household indebtedness relative to disposable income rose from almost 100% in 1997 to 140% in 2006. Figure 3.2 compares the evolution of home prices to income and household indebtedness in the US compared to a number of OECD countries.

The credit boom manifested itself in the growth of banking assets which rose to represent 100% of US GDP in 2007, up from 81% in 2001, from USD9.1 trillion to USD13.8 trillion. Debt capital markets to GDP grew from 186% of GDP in 2001 to 234% of GDP in 2007, rising from USD18.2 trillion to USD31 trillion.

3.2 US Sub–Prime Crisis (2006–2007 and Beyond)

From June 2004 to August 2007, the Federal Reserve had hiked rates from 1% to 5.75% (high of 6.25% in June 2006) in a series of successive raises. At the same time, the portion of subprime mortgage lending had risen to capture around 20% of total mortgage lending. In 2006 lenders extended USD640 billion in subprime mortgages – three times the levels of 2003. These securities were packaged and repackaged into several mortgage-backed securities and sold to investors in the US and internationally, after being 'credit' enhanced using various tools, whether they be insurance guarantees or other methodologies. Typically, subprime mortgage lending would involve low initial teaser rates, with a later repricing to a benchmark such as the federal funds rate. Thus, borrowers were hit by two factors: their own mortgages repricing and the benchmark rate rising significantly. As a result, almost 13 percent of subprime loans became delinquent, more than five times the delinquency rate for home loans to borrowers with top credit and more than 2 percent of subprime loans had foreclosure proceedings start in the fourth quarter of 2007.

In January 2007, mortgage brokers Ownit Solutions filed for bankruptcy, with reportedly USD93 million owed to Merrill Lynch. A month later Mortgage Lenders Network USA Inc also filed for bankruptcy. Mortgage Lenders Network was the 15th largest subprime lender in the US, with USD3.3 billion in loans extended in the 3Q06. Other lenders followed suit, filing for bankruptcy over February and March 2007 including Accredited Home Lenders Holding, DR Horton and Countrywide Financial. The latter is depicted in Michael Moore's *Capitalism: A Love Story* which chronicles how the companies advertised their products and the type of borrower they sought, an insight into how this industry sub-sector functioned. In April of that year, New Century Financial, the largest subprime lender in the US, filed for bankruptcy, after having extended some USD60 billion in mortgage loans in 2006.

Over the summer of 2007 financial investors in subprime mortgage securities began to suffer. In June, Bear Stearns halted redemptions on two of its funds, the High-Grade Structured Credit Strategies Enhanced Leverage Fund and the High-Grade Structured Credit Fund. This was followed by BNP Paribas in August suspending redemptions from three investment funds that invested in subprime mortgage debt, due to a 'complete evaporation of liquidity' in the market. The Fed's efforts to increase market liquidity through direct injections and a 50 bps cut in August to 5.75% and another 50 bps in September to 5.25% were unsuccessful.

It wasn't long before banks started announcing direct hits to their balance sheets, an avalanche of rising loss figures from USD5.5 billion by Merrill Lynch in October 2007, shortly revised to USD8.4 billion a couple of weeks later in 3Q07 losses, with other major players following suit across the globe. Total losses booked in 3Q07 amounted to a hefty USD72 billion and in 4Q07 USD89 billion. Combined these losses eroded 10% of the equity of the banks reporting these losses. Some USD20 billion more in losses were reported in the 1Q08 and the market estimated that a further USD400 billion (Morgan Stanley and Goldman Sachs) to USD600 billion (UBS) more losses are to be realized – the latter loss figure represented 37% of total bank capital of the largest 30 financial institutions around the world. Although banks attempted to boost their capital in 4Q07, the USD24 billion raised from sovereign wealth funds (SWFs) proved to be nothing more than a drop in the ocean. A proposal by some of the banks to set up a USD100 billion super fund to invest in mortgage securities was withdrawn after it became obvious that this was not just a short-term liquidity crisis, but a structural one.

3.3 US Bank and NBFI Failures and Confidence Crisis (September 2008 and Beyond)

With the ongoing disruption of wholesale money markets, Bear Stearns collapsed in March 2008 followed by Lehman Brothers in September. Bear Stearns was granted an emergency loan of USD30 billion by JP Morgan Chase in March in conjunction with the Fed and later acquired by the bank for a consideration of USD1.2 billion or USD10 per share, up from an initial offer of USD2 per share or consideration of USD240 million – far below the 52-week high for the stock of USD133 per share. The acquisition was agreed upon by JP Morgan only after the Fed agreed to assume some of Bear Stearns' most toxic assets, including its holdings of some Countrywide securities, which the Fed assumed as part of its Maiden Lane portfolio. Bear Stearns was the fifth-largest investment bank in the US. At the end of fiscal year 2007, Bear Stearns had a net equity position of only USD11.1 billion and USD395 billion in assets, indicating a leverage ratio of 35.5 to 1.

In *House of Cards: A Tale of Hubris and Wretched Excess on Wall Street* William Cohan describes the president of Atlantic Advisors, a USD3.5 billion investment management company and hedge fund, telling his clients about huge problems at Bear Stearns and Lehman Brothers, in the form of 'nuclear waste' on their balance sheets, huge inventories of securities backed by home mortgages. He speaks of a double whammy to these banks: defaults on the mortgages and falling value of underlying collateral – namely people's homes.

Lehman's collapse was the turning point that prompted a complete market loss of confidence and led the three largest remaining US investment banks to sell themselves to, or become, depository institutions. Cohan also talks about how, before its collapse, Lehman had increased its leverage from 25 times to 35 times, announced a large stock buyback at USD65 and then sold stock at USD38 shortly after, an indication of serious mismanagement. More importantly, Lehman's bankruptcy spread default risk and removed an important financial counterparty, sharply reducing liquidity in the derivatives markets. What began as a *liquidity crisis* transformed into a *solvency crisis*.

This was followed by the insurance conglomerate AIG nearly collapsing, raising broader concerns about financial product insurance and instigating a public sector rescue to the tune of USD85 billion in the form of a credit line (later total assistance to AIG by the US government reached almost USD180 billion by May 2009). In November 2008, the US government agreed to protect USD306 billion worth of loans and securities on Citigroup's books and to inject USD20 billion of cash in return for a USD27 billion preferred equity stake. See Appendix for more details.

3.4 Global Bank and NBFI Failures (January 2008 and Beyond)

The first institution to show signs of distress in Europe was the German regional bank Sachsen which was subsequently sold to competitors in September 2007. A number of other European banks, such as Société Générale, IKB and UBS, had announced sizable losses in the summer of 2007, but could not foresee the magnitude of the crisis that followed in 2008. A number of banks and non-bank financial institutions were either sold or bailed out directly by their governments.

On 28 September, 2008, the governments of Belgium, Luxembourg and the Netherlands bailed out and part-nationalized the insurance company

Fortis and its banking arm, followed by the bank, Dexia, which was rescued by the Benelux governments and France. Both institutions had a large presence in the Benelux and neighbouring region with a bailout of 11.2 billion euros for Fortis and 6.4 billion euros for Dexia. By the end of September, Ireland announced a blanket guarantee on all deposits in its national banks (including those operating abroad). Germany, Denmark, Greece and Sweden followed suit in the first week of October. The German government on 6 October bailed out Hypo Real Estate (HRE), one of Germany's biggest banking conglomerates, at a cost of 50 billion euros. This was followed by a coordinated interest rate cut of 50 basis points on 8 October by the US Federal Reserve, the European Central Bank, the Bank of Canada, the central banks of Sweden and Switzerland and the Bank of England.

By 11 October all the Eurozone governments decided to part-nationalize their financial systems. More specifically, they agreed to guarantee nearly all debts and interbank lending, and provide funding for the recapitalization of banks that voluntarily participated in the scheme. In addition, France and Germany imposed stringent conditions on executive pay or bonuses. Overall, the National Economic Institute Review provided estimates that funding to resurrect the wholesale money market could reach *1,125 billion* euros in the Eurozone. Although Germany has pledged 100 billion euros so far for recapitalization and debt guarantees, it has made clear that it is willing to inject up to 400 billion euros into its financial system. Little did it know that it might also be called upon to support other financial systems in the Euro area at the time, such as Greece. Figure 3.3 shows the various bailout packages by selected European governments.

In the UK, Northern Rock, the UK's fifth-largest mortgage lender, was nationalized in the 1Q2008, after exploring the option of private sale. Depositors panicked on the back of global subprime mortgage troubles and withdrew GBP1.0 billion (or around 4% of the bank's deposit base) in one day. Initially, the terms of the bailout were that the Bank of England provides an open-ended facility to Northern Rock, allowing it to access liquidity by posting mortgages or mortgage-backed securities as collateral. Surprisingly, at the time, Northern Rock's bad debts stood below industry average of 1%. So what triggered the run? The bank's business model resulted in a high-risk profile, rendering the bank vulnerable in the case of a crisis because of a) high growth in lending with gross loans booking GBP19.3 billion in 1H07, up from GBP14.8 billion in 1H06. Growth was propelled partially by Northern Rock granting loans with a loan-to-value (LTV) of more than 100% for the first time, up from 78% in the 1H07) and b) the bank's funding mix as of June 2007 was 25.5% *non-retail deposits* which are cheaper than retail deposits, but are also *less stable.*

Figure 3.3. Bailout Packages in the Eurozone (Euros).*

	Debt Guarantees	Recapitalization	Other	Conditions
France	320 billion for new debt issuance	40 billion	Deposit guarantee up to 70,000	Cap on pay and bonuses
Germany	Up to 400 billion for bad debt, of which 20 billion to cover potential credit guarantee losses	70 billion	10 billion to buy troubled assets	Cap on executive pay (500,000) and ban on bonuses
Spain	100 billion for new debt in 2008			
Italy			Up to 40 billion in treasury bills to improve liquidity and refinancing	
Austria	85 billion for bank lending	15 billion		Ban on short selling
Netherlands	200 billion for interbank lending	20 billion		
Belgium			Deposit guarantee raised to 100,000	
Ireland			400 billion for all banking liabilities	
Portugal	20 billion for interbank debt		Deposit guarantee raised to 100,000	
Euro Area	Up to 1125 billion	Up to 145 billion		

*Schemes announced up to 16 October, 2008.
Source: *National Institute Economic Review* No. 206, October, 2008.

So it was not, as erroneously believed, trouble in the UK housing market that triggered Northern Rock's woes, it was its business model and the funding crunch which resulted from the housing market troubles in the US. In their book *The Gods that Failed*, Larry Elliott and Dan Atkinson present an interesting quote by Adam Applegarth, chief executive of Northern Rock, taken from the *Independent* on September 16, 2007, 'as a cashier I was particularly inept because I could never get the tills to balance'.

Following the demise of Northern Rock, mortgage lender Bradford and Bingley collapsed in September 2008 and Santander paid GBP612 million for its branches and deposits, Lloyds TSB and RBS became part-nationalized (the UK government currently owns 43% and 70% respectively in each bank). Lloyds TSB acquired HBOS in September 2008 for a consideration of GBP12.2 billion.

In October 2008 the UK authorities announced a comprehensive support package, including capital injections, for UK-incorporated banks and guarantees for new short- to medium-term senior unsecured bank debt. The plan provides for several sources of funding to be made available, to an aggregate total of GBP500 billion in loans and guarantees. This includes GBP200 billion to be made available for short-term loans through the Bank of England's Special Liquidity Scheme. Secondly, the government will support British banks in their plan to increase their market capitalization through the newly formed Bank Recapitalization Fund, by GBP25 billion in the first instance with a further GBP25 billion to be called upon if needed. Thirdly, the government will temporarily underwrite any eligible lending between British banks, giving a loan guarantee of around GBP250 billion, with all banks incorporated in the UK and building societies being eligible to access the programme. The UK government subsequently announced that some GBP60 billion would go towards supporting banking sector capitalization, including the amounts injected in both Lloyds and RBS.

Icelandic Banks suffered from a full-fledged collapse in 2008 which spilled over to the real economy with GDP falling 65% in euro terms (taking into account exchange rate drops vis-à-vis the euro). Iceland saw its three major banks (Landsbanki, Kaupthing and Glitner) collapse in the same week in October 2008. The UK has used anti-terror laws against the Icelandic government, with the result that there are capital controls in Iceland, multiple exchange rates for the krona, and Iceland seeks to refloat its currency with IMF help. Among the causes of the crisis in Iceland according to Danielsson (2008) are: a peculiar central bank governance structure which seems to lack impartiality and an oversized banking sector with Icelandic banks having foreign assets of around *11 times Iceland's GDP before the crisis* (loss estimates to foreign creditors of the Icelandic crisis hover around a total of USD40 billion). One bank, Landsbanki (through its Icesave entity), offered interest rates much higher than the market, attracting some GBP4.5 billion in the UK and around GBP1.0 billion in the Netherlands in deposits (losses are estimated at GBP5.0 billion, the amount in the Icelandic deposit insurance fund only covers a small fraction). Iceland has since requested a USD2.0 billion loan from the IMF and a USD4.0 billion loan from its Nordic neighbours.

3.5 Impact on Global Real Macro-Performance (2008 and Beyond)

Clearly the 2007–10 crisis and beyond will have a huge impact on the global macro-economic stage, business models of financial and non-financial firms, financial and non-financial agents, regulation, government finance and almost every aspect of the economy. This impact will manifest itself in global output losses, a credit crunch, deleveraging of the global economy, more bankruptcies in industries (automotives were the first to suffer followed by commercial real estate losses, all triggering another wave of banking losses) and contagion to emerging markets.

Over the past century, the global economy shifted from a manufacturing-led to a services-led economy, with finance at the forefront. The size of the financial sector and its relationship with other sectors grew to the extent that all aspects of economic activity were linked to the financial sector in one way or another. In 2007 OECD countries, which capture three-quarters of global GDP, financial sector assets (the total of banking sector assets, equity and debt market capitalization and pension and insurance assets, on-balance sheet and reported activity components alone, not OTC) averaged 490% of GDP, up from 300% in 2000. This ratio was 972% in Ireland, 968% in the UK, 706% in Spain, 664% in the US, 640% in Australia and 508% in Japan. What does the financial sector 'create' such that it commands multiples of GDP as these? As the sector deflates, the structure of the global economy will not only shrink but will have to change dramatically.

Portugal, Italy, Greece and Spain (PIGS), which suffer from large macro imbalances and are thereby seen as the weakest links in developed Europe, were affected by *'financial'* contagion. The impact of the direct write-downs taken by banks and other non-bank financial institutions, however, was nowhere close to the magnitude of the impact the shift in global risk premiums and drying up of liquidity in international markets has had on these countries. Write-downs will not recur with this magnitude, but could continue in a slow-bleed manner as the global economy shrinks and deleverages. The impact on the ability of these countries to roll over their external funding and how much they pay for that funding constitutes a structural shift which has threatened bankruptcy in the case of Greece and led to downgrades for the group as a whole. Greece had some USD29 billion of debt to be rolled over in 2010 alone – that is almost 10% of its estimated GDP in 2010 and the terms on its debt issued up to the first quarter of 2010 were 300bps above the German Bund – if we say they raise USD30 billion, then this translates into additional interest of USD900 million per annum. The funding problem for these markets caps a plethora of macro imbalances which give them very little room for manoeuvre in the form of high budget deficits (Greece at 13% of GDP for example), high unemployment rates and high public debt to GDP ratios.

For emerging markets, contagion effects have been mild and mainly through *trade* channels. Given the size of Asia's holdings of USD8.0 trillion of loans and securities, the low cumulative expected loss rates of 2.1% estimated by the IMF suggests either that the continent was much more prudent in its investment decisions or that this loss rate is underestimated. The squeeze was and will be felt through the trade channel however – as consumers they also deleverage, not just corporates. In 2008 the US imported USD338 billion of goods from China, equivalent to 8% of China's GDP of USD4.4 trillion. With slowing global growth, emerging markets dependent on exports will have to change their business models.

Brazil, Russia, India, China (BRICs) are also susceptible to contagion through the trade channel. In September 2008, Russia lent the country's three biggest banks, Sberbank, VTB Bank and Gazprombank, 1.13 trillion roubles (USD44 billion) for at least three months to boost liquidity. The Central Bank lowered the reserve requirement, raising the cap for deposit insurance from 400 to 700 thousand rubles (USD25,000).

Of Central and Eastern Europe, the Middle East and Africa (CEMEA) and Central and Eastern Europe (CEE) regions, the latter has suffered the most. The CEE has a small population base of around 120 million people spread over 15 countries. Collectively, these nations had a GDP of USD1.2 trillion in 2007. Countries such as Latvia, Lithuania, Estonia and Romania had seen significant growth in their banking sector assets over the last decade, with international banks establishing a presence in their markets and moving to control a substantial portion of assets. Moreover, it was common practice that these foreign banks extended foreign currency loans to corporates and individuals who did not have the ability to hedge these risks. With the credit boom, real estate bubbles developed all over the region. Latvia in particular had a huge commercial real estate overhang, asking the IMF and the EU for an emergency bailout loan of 7.5 billion euros in February 2009, while at the same time the government nationalized Parex Bank, the country's second-largest bank. The government coalition headed by Prime Minister Ivars Godmanis collapsed. This shows that for really vulnerable economies, financial crises could spill over into 'political' crises. The 1980s movie *Roll Over* starring Jane Fonda portrayed riots in countries on the back of a financial meltdown in the US. Is life inspired by movies or are movies inspired by life? Sometimes we cannot really tell.

In the Middle East and North Africa (MENA) region bailout measures announced by governments totalled USD113 billion, ranging from 3% of GDP in Saudi Arabia to a hefty 44% in Kuwait, or 9% of the region's total GDP. In addition, indirect output losses were estimated at 2.2% of regional GDP over the years 2009–11. For these countries the main culprit was financial contagion. The IMF estimates that each one percentage point increase in a financial stress index (FSI) in advanced economies results in 0.3% increase in MENA countries FSI and up to 0.5% drop in GDP.

Over the past five years, there was substantial evolution in countries such as the UAE and Qatar, which both developed financial centres. The Dubai International Financial Centre (DIFC) in particular was a huge success, with the number of registered companies rising exponentially. By the end of August 2009, DIFC had more than 850 companies listed and several had chosen Dubai as its regional headquarters. The DIFC caters to the Middle East as a region, with its population of 200 million, a combined economy of USD1.8 trillion and annual GDP growth rates in excess of 5%. Dubai is one of seven Emirates in the UAE built on trade and financial services, it doesn't have access to the oil resources its rich neighbour the emirate of Abu Dhabi does. The population of the UAE is estimated at 6 million, of which the Emiratis comprise only 20%, the rest being foreign nationals. Given this backdrop, Dubai's economy flourished propelled by trade and financial services, which in turn developed as a result of a huge reliance on leverage. The stock market was trading at insane multiples (leverage of 10 to 1 at one point in time was prevalent on margin trades) and loan to value (LTV) ratios on mortgages were north of 100%, with a huge number of extravagant development projects and high-sale prices per square foot. When the financial crisis resulted in layoffs across global banks, including in Dubai, a large number of people simply took off and left the country, defaulting on their mortgages and leaving their cars, bought on credit, at the airport. Banks and real estate developers were left with these exposures on their books, which is why I believe that reported non-performing loans for this region still do not reflect the reality of the situation and the drop in collateral asset values.

In November 2009, Dubai World, a real estate company with operations in more than 100 countries and debts in excess of USD59 billion, announced it wanted to delay payments on some USD26 billion owed to creditors, including HSBC and Standard Chartered Bank, thus there was reverse credit-risk transfer from the region to developed markets. In December 2009, the rich emirate of Abu Dhabi granted USD10 billion in aid to Dubai World, of which it said it would use USD4.1 billion to repay its subsidiary's (Nakheel) Islamic bond maturing on the same day. Qatar has a similar profile for both the financial markets and margin trading and an even worse real estate bubble. Neither of them have fully burst – yet.

In North Africa, banking sectors have been seeing stagnant growth over the past decade, with loans-to-deposits ratios falling to as low as 55% in Egypt for example, and significant excess 'lending' capacity in the region as a whole. Yet paradoxically there is a regional credit crunch as banks continue to provide captive funding for government and hold large positions in treasuries, earning easy money and not providing funding badly needed by small and medium sized enterprises (SME's). These countries had limited exposure to 'toxic' assets so to speak and to counterparty risk with the likes of Bear Stearns and Lehman, simply because of size: they were too small to be affected by having allocated investments as such, while treasury and derivative markets are underdeveloped, so again there was limited counterparty exposure. These countries nonetheless saw their own real estate bubbles get bigger, however, and their reported non-performing loans are understated on the back of overly optimistic cash flow expectations for the corporate sector in a global economic slowdown and not taking into account developer failures and construction project cancellations in the near term.

In Sub-Saharan Africa (SSA), a similar scenario is unfolding, but without the real estate component: very small banking sectors. As such there are advantages to underdevelopment – the question is: on their path to growth, will these countries bear in mind lessons from this current crisis? More importantly, will they avoid complacency about their own problems which include fundamental credit quality issues, governance and poor intermediation, among others.

Chapter 4

SYSTEMIC AND INSTITUTIONAL COST OF THE 2007–10 CRISIS

In *Too Big to Fail* Andrew Sorkin gives the account of a conference call between Jamie Dimon, chairman and chief executive officer of JP Morgan, and two dozen members of his management team on 13 September, 2008, the weekend before Lehman Brothers filed for bankruptcy and a night after Dimon met at the New York Fed with a number of his peers on Wall Street. He tells them '... this is a matter of life and death...we need to prepare right now for Lehman Brothers filing...and for AIG filing...and for Merrill Lynch filing...and for Morgan Stanley filing... and potentially for Goldman Sachs filing.' This is one of the definitions of a systemic crisis as opposed to a banking failure where just one bank is in trouble – it's a crisis for an *entire* system. This chapter attempts to put the events of the past few years in context compared to previous crises, highlight similarities and differences and discuss the various impacts these events have had on the global macro-economic picture and the outlook for the future. The chapter explores the way in which business models of financial and non-financial firms, financial and non-financial agents, regulation, government finance and almost every aspect of economic activity are affected. The first section defines what constitutes a systemic financial crisis; section two is a discussion of output costs (i.e. losses to GDP of direct bailouts and of potential GDP which could have been produced but was not because of the impact a crisis has on the real economy); section three looks at agent losses (i.e write-downs by different players); section four investigates the crisis outlook covering various channels of contagion to emerging markets; and section five covers the outlook with regards to the real economy and various market segments.

4.1 Definition of Systemic Financial Crises

What constitutes a systemic financial crisis and why was the past crisis classified as such? The Lehman Brothers example illustrates the concept of a serial or 'domino' theory default. The largest database of global crises was presented by Reinhart and Rogoff (2008) in a paper which offers a panoramic description of the history of financial crises starting from England's fourteenth century default, it finds that serial default is an almost universal phenomenon. The paper, which was later developed into a book, finds that the US subprime crisis is not unique and points to the fallacy of adopting a 'this time it is different' approach. The authors also document other crises that often accompany default including inflation, exchange rate crashes and banking crises. Prior to the 2007 crisis, widely used definitions of a *systemic* crisis were the Demirgüç-Kunt and Detragiache (1998) and the Caprio and Klingebiel (1996) definitions whereby a systemic crisis is identified if any of the following criteria apply:

1. Proportion of NPLs to total banking system assets is greater than 10%;
2. Public bailout costs exceed 2% of GDP;
3. Systemic crisis causes large-scale bank nationalization;
4. Extensive bank runs are visible or an emergency government intervention is required;
5. 'All or most of banking capital is exhausted'; and
6. The level of non-performing loans falls between 5% and 10% or less if subjectively deemed systemically significant.

While Kaminsky and Reinhart (1999) use similar criteria, with a crisis considered systemic if bank runs result in closure or nationalization of at least one bank, or if there are no runs then large-scale government intervention, or merging or nationalization of one bank are followed by a domino effect on other banks. Lindgren et al (1996) define a systemic crisis on the basis of whether bank runs, portfolio shifts, bank collapses or large-scale government intervention occur. Any other episodes of financial instability are classified as non-systemic crises.

4.2 Output Costs

4.2.1 Output Costs of Past Crises

The most recent crisis has a total estimated toll of about USD14.0 trillion (USD3.4 trillion direct write-downs and USD10.2 trillion in 'lost' GDP or GDP opportunity cost), this represents almost a ***quarter*** of estimated global GDP in 2010. Davis & Karim (2003) identify cost of systemic crises as both *direct bailouts cost* and *indirect in terms of GDP costs*. Caprio and Klingebiel (1996) find bailouts cost on average 10% of GDP, with some crises much more costly like the Mexican Tequila Crisis (1994) which cost 20% of GDP, and the Jamaican crisis (1996) which had a toll equivalent to 37% of GDP. Hoggarth, Reis and Saporta (2002) find that the cumulative output losses from banking and twin crises averaged 23.8% for OECD economies, compared to 13.9% in emerging economies, while banking crises cost an average of 5.6% of GDP and twin crises 29.9%, respectively. Hoggarth and Reidhill (2003) and Heffernan (2007) identify output losses as a percentage of real GDP, where output losses are defined as the cumulative deviation in the level of output from its pre-crisis 10-year trend. Finally, Honohan (2008) finds that costs of systemic crises could range from 10% in the lower quartile to 30% in the upper quartile based on 78 systemic crises as identified by Caprio and Klingebiel et al. (2005). Barrell, Hurst and Kirby (2008) estimate the cost of the Japanese banking crises to be at almost 72% of GDP in terms of output loss. Figure 4.1 illustrates output costs to GDP for different crisis episodes.

4.2.2 Output Costs of the Current Crisis

According to an update on the IMF's World Economic Outlook released in January 2009, world growth is projected to fall to a mere 0.5% percent, the lowest rate since World War II, with significant financial strains remaining acute. Cumulative (indirect) output losses over 2008–10 are estimated at

Figure 4.1. Output Losses of Financial Crises as a % of GDP (1980–2002) and in Major Crisis Episodes to Date.

Country	Year	Cost (% of GDP)
Argentina	1980-1982	55
Argentina	1995	2
Mexico	1995-1997	14
Brazil	1995	5-10
Chile	1981-1983	41
Cote D'Ivoire^	1988-1991	25
China**	1990s	47
Indonesia**	1997-1999	50-60
Korea	1997-1999	15
Thailand	1997-1999	24
Malaysia	1997-1999	10
Philippines**	1998-2000	7
Russia**	1998	5-7
Spain**	1977-1985	17
Finland	1991-1993	8-10
Norway	1988-1992	4
Sweden	1991-1993	4-5
US (thrifts bailout)	1984-1991	5-7
Japan*	1990-2002	17-20

(*Continued*)

Figure 4.1. Continued.

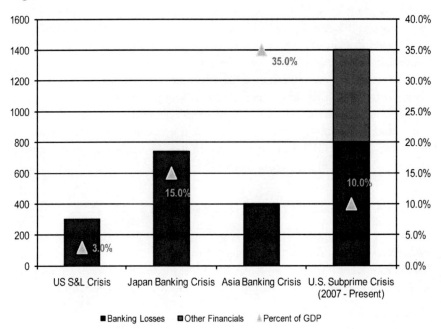

Sources: Evans (2000), Heffernan (2002).
*BIS (2004) estimates the total cost of dealing with Japan's non-performing loans between April 1992 and September 2001 was 20% of GDP.
**Beim and Calomiris (2001). BIS (2001). ^1999.
Presentation by James Bullard, CEO, Federal Reserve Bank of St. Louis, 4 December, 2008. Washington University in St. Louis, Olin Business School.

around 5% of global output (this amounts to USD10.2 trillion if we apply the rate to IMF global output estimates). Most of the loss in output is forecast to take place in developed countries which could likely see their output drop collectively by 6%, while emerging markets are predicted to see a drop of around 4%. However, it seems that the IMF is calibrating these expectations based on previously experienced crises since the 1970s, which could potentially mean that these forecasts, in my opinion, are underestimating the impact of the current crisis given the much higher level of leverage and complexity at the onset of this crisis compared to previous downturns.

4.3 Agent Losses

The IMF's total estimate of losses was revised significantly upwards in April 2009 to USD4.0 trillion (up from USD1.45 trillion in April 2008 and USD945 million in January 2008) and down again in October 2009 to USD3.4 trillion. Actual losses realized thus far by financial institutions globally amounted to USD1.9 trillion (USD760 billion in September 2008, of which USD580 billion are by banks). Are we to see the rest of these losses materialize?

If we classify the losses into: a) losses which have already been realized; b) losses still to be realized, have been estimated in magnitude but their timing is uncertain; and c) losses which are unknown in size and are yet to materialize at an unknown timing. It is this last leg which creates the greatest uncertainty and comprises the biggest risk of further self-fulfilling losses being realized. Figure 4.2 represents these different categories and the potential hidden 'iceberg' of losses yet to be realized. This presentation and identification of the potential spillover into other credit market sub-segments and to other financial sector players was shown *as early as August 2007* by briefing reports of the Macroprudential Unit at the Central Bank of Egypt. This breakdown is clearly linked to the relative importance of the different components of the financial markets, with total derivatives standing at around USD746.9 trillion in June 2008, of which only USD59.8 trillion is exchange traded (CDS outstanding estimated at USD60 trillion, respectively). The longer plans for a central clearing house for OTC derivatives drag on without materializing, the worse the uncertainty and potential losses to be realized.

Figure 4.2. 'Iceberg' of Financial Sector Losses.

Sources: Macro-Prudential Unit Analysis. January 2008. FT, Bloomberg, Company Announcements & Financial Releases.
Please refer to the Annex for more details.
*UBS estimates at USD600 billion. Goldman Sachs estimates at USD1.2 trillion in March 2008, respectively.

Source: N Saleh, Presentation at Al-Mal 2nd Annual Stock Market Conference, Cairo, Egypt, 12 April, 2008.

4.3.1 Banks

Following on from the discussion in Chapter 3 and the examples given, losses by banks globally on the back of securities write-downs amounted to around USD600 billion as of end of 2008, with Citigroup booking around a *tenth* of these losses. By mid-2009, this figure had jumped to USD1.3 trillion, with an outlook for total losses to tally some USD3.4 trillion or more over the coming two years. The impact on the global capitalization of the banking system was a watershed, losing more than two thirds of its value from January 2007 to 31 March, 2009, as illustrated by Figure 4.3.

The pace of losses quickened following the collapse of Lehman Brothers in September 2008. Losses at Lehman's also moved at an alarming rate, starting with only USD0.7 billion in write-downs in September 2007, and swelling to USD3.2 billion in March 2008, USD8.3 billion in June and USD13.5 billion

Figure 4.3. Write-Downs by Major Banks and Market Capitalization of the Global Banking Sector Post-Crisis.

Bank	Country	USD Billion
Citigroup	USA	60.8
Wachovia	USA	52.7
Merrill Lynch	USA	52.2
Washington Mutual	USA	45.6
UBS	CHE	44.2
HSBC	GBR	27.4
Bank of America	USA	21.2
JPMorgan Chase	USA	18.8
Morgan Stanley	USA	15.7
IKB	DEU	14.3
Royal Bank of Scotland	GBR	13.8
Lehman Brothers	USA	13.8
Deutsche Bank	DEU	10.1
Credit Suisse	CHE	10.1
Wells Fargo	USA	10
Credit Agricole	FRA	8.6
Barclays	GBR	7.5
Canadian Imperial (CIBC)	CAN	7.1
Fortis	BEL/NLD	6.9
Bayerische Landesbank	DEU	6.7
HBOS	GBR	6.6
ING Group	NLD	6.5
Societe Generale	FRA	6.4
Mizuho Financial	JPN	6.1
Sub-Total		**473.1**
Worldwide		**586.2**

(Continued)

Figure 4.3. Continued.

Country	Market Cap (USD Billion)	
	Jan 1 2007	Mar 31 2009
Argentina	9.2	3.7
Australia	225.7	139.7
Belgium	184.6	17
Brazil	250	206
Canada	236.7	135.1
China	667.4	525.3
France	372.8	97.8
Germany	151.6	37
Hong Kong	345.8	131.5
India	60.4	41.1
Indonesia	30.9	24.8
Ireland	53.9	1.2
Italy	338.1	99.3
Japan	651.3	248.8
Mexico	24.4	23.3
Netherlands	22.7	1.8
Poland	51.2	20.2
Portugal	38.3	10.4
Russia	126	23.9
Singapore	68.3	34.5
South Africa	48.2	33
Spain	306.2	112
Sweden	108.4	39.3
Switzerland	281.9	81.3
UK	714.4	163.3
US	1560.5	352.1
Total	**6,929**	**2,603**

Source: Honohan, 2008, FT 1 April 2009.

in September of that year (totalling USD27.0 billion over the period), while capital injections had amounted to USD29.0 billion. Following the demise of Lehman's, Merrill Lynch accepted a purchase offer by Bank of America with a price tag of around USD50 billion, a huge drop from its capitalization a year earlier of about USD100 billion.

4.3.1a Outlook for Write-Downs and Provisioning by Region

The US has the highest expected cumulative loss rates of 8.2%; it has already booked USD654 billion in write-downs on loans with some USD371 billion in estimated losses on securities which have materialized but are yet to be booked on bank balance sheets from mid-2009 to the end of 2010. Figure 4.4 compares the US, the UK, Europe and other regions and shows

Figure 4.4. Write-Downs on Bank Holdings of Loans and Securities and Expected Loss Rates by Region.

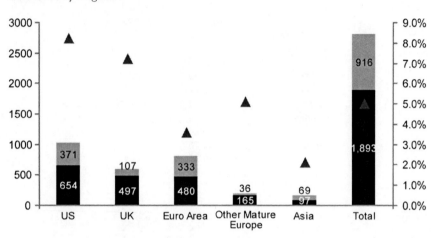

Other mature Europe includes Denmark, Iceland, Norway, Sweden and Switzerland. Asia includes Australia, Hong Kong SAR, Japan, New Zealand and Singapore.
Source: IMF GFSR, October 2009.

that there is a sizable portion of losses yet to be booked in the UK and the Eurozone, while the US is ahead in the cycle. In total, USD1,893 billion in global losses on loans have been booked and USD916 billion are yet to be booked, with a cumulative expected loss rate of 5%. Given the size of its holdings of USD8.0 trillion of loans and securities in Asia, the low cumulative expected loss rates of 2.1%, is by far the lowest compared to other regions, which could possibly be explained by regional market segmentation premises, better risk management, or alternatively, these loss rates could well be underestimated.

4.3.1b Capital Raised by Banks

In November 2007, when the crisis was still more or less confined to the US, Citigroup managed to raise USD7.5 billion through the sale of preferred capital, convertible to a 4.9% equity stake, to the Abu Dhabi Investment Authority (ADIA), one of the world's largest sovereign wealth funds with estimated assets of USD875 billion. Since then, the amount of capital raised by banks has been staggering. According to the IMF's Global Financial Stability Report (GFSR) in October of 2009, major global banking players raised USD930 billion in fresh capital from crisis inception up to 2Q09. Sovereign wealth funds (SWFs had a total estimated capital of around USD3.0 trillion in 2008) contributed USD80 billion to these capital raisings, up from USD24 billion in the early stages of the crisis in 2007. In the US, USD500 billion has been raised to date, USD220 billion in the Eurozone, mostly by UK banks that have raised in total more than USD160 billion, and more than USD50 billion in other mature European countries including Denmark, Iceland, Norway, Sweden and Switzerland.

The question is whether this will be sufficient or not, as the sector deleverages to pre-crisis levels. In the UK, for example, Gieve (2009) states that median leverage of UK banks in 2006 was 10.0 times; in 2008 this stood at 20.0 times (measured as total assets/total equity less minority interest). Where will the balance come from to compensate for the reduction in leverage if we go back to 2006 levels? Gieve conjectures that the deleveraging will be partly achieved through asset sales, slower new asset growth and significant changes to banks' business models as several revenue sources which existed prior to the crisis are no longer in place, nor are they likely to reappear in the medium term. Please refer to Figure 2.8 in Chapter 2 for the impact of deleveraging on bank RoA and RoE in various regions. For additional capital raising requirements, the IMF estimates, based on three scenarios of different target minimum capital ratios by banks by year end 2010 additional capital needs of USD180 billion on the low end (based on an assumption of a low minimum capital ratio required), to USD530 billion in the mid-range (based on an assumption of a moderate minimum capital ratio required) and USD670 billion in the high range (based on an assumption of a high minimum capital ratio required), with the majority of these capital needs are estimated to be in the Eurozone.

4.3.1c Refinancing Needs of Banks are High in the Near Term

The IMF estimates that over 2009 and the first quarter of 2010, the largest global banks face debt funding needs of over *USD700 billion*. Eurozone banks still rely heavily on wholesale funding markets and thus will face huge refinancing requirements in 2009 and 2010. Hence, any further market shocks, such as the public debt crisis overhang in Europe, poses serious threats to the refinancing operations and their terms. Banks might not be able to roll over the funding they require, or they might have to pay much more than they expected for it.

For the UK, according to analyses undertaken by the Bank of England and Fathom Consulting, funding needs are forecast to peak in 2011 and 2012, with some GBP650 billion-plus in net liabilities to be refinanced based on maturity ladders of existing funding.

4.3.2 Insurance Companies

The first types of insurer to be affected were mono-lines (mostly US-based bond insurers which include MBIA and Ambac and which had collectively incurred USD20 billion losses in the past crisis). A ratings downgrade not only stops a mono-line from undertaking new business, it would probably lead to a downgrade in all debt the insurance company has guaranteed, and in turn trigger another spiral of losses in the value of these investments for their holders. This was indeed the case for some of the Maiden Lane (Bear Stearns) assets that the Fed assumed, resulting in significant losses to this portfolio. The Fed had initially refused to release details of this portfolio, was sued by Bloomberg and forced to disclose them in April of 2010. Bloomberg had estimated that lower ratings for mono-lines could impact debt worth USD2.4 trillion if they materialize, potentially causing losses of as much as USD200 billion.

MBIA secured USD1.0 billion funding commitment from Warburg Pincus at the end of 2007, the US private equity group. However, analysts had estimated that MBIA will need at least an additional USD2.0 billion in order to guarantee its Triple-A rating. It then completed an offering which increased its claims-paying resources by as much as USD3.2 billion in approximately two months. Nevertheless, MBIA's credit rating was downgraded from AAA to AA, by S&P in June 2008, and BB+ in 3Q09.

Ambac, which is about half the size of MBIA in terms of total assets, announced plans to raise USD1.5 billion in equity in 1Q2008. It made a public offering of USD1.155 billion in March 2008 and also placed 14,074,074 shares of common stock in a private placement for USD95 million with two financial institutions. In addition, Ambac also completed its USD250 million public offering of 5 million equity units, with a stated amount of USD50 per unit. Nevertheless it still got downgraded four notches in November, 2008 from Aa3 to Baa1, and in 3Q09 to junk status by S&P (CC−).

Insurance giant AIG incurred a hefty USD100 billion in losses in 2008 (in Q4 alone USD61.7 billion) and has received US government aid to the tune of USD180 billion up to May 2009 USD85 billion of which was in exchange for warrants for 79.9% of the equity of AIG. According to AIG, its biggest counterparties for credit default swaps and securities lending for the last quarter of 2008 comprised Goldman Sachs, Société Générale, Deutsche Bank, Barclays, Merrill Lynch, Bank of America, UBS and BNP, for a total of around USD70 billion. These counterparts were the main beneficiaries of AIG's bailout.

European insurer Swiss Re announced losses of USD1.0 billion on two complex credit default swaps (CDS), Munich Re announced USD220 million, and Allianz announced USD851 million, in 2007. The bailout of CIFG,

French investment bank's Natixis bond insurance arm, is the first for a specialist insurance group – a mono-line – that writes guarantees for debt issuers. USD1.5 billion was pledged by two French banks, Caisse D'Epargne and Banque Populaire, to support CIFG's Triple-A rating. Natixis had booked USD603 million in losses, reducing profits for the 3Q07 by almost a third, on the back of the subprime crisis.

4.4 Crisis Outlook

4.4.1 What are the Risks of Contagion to Emerging Markets and are they Quantifiable?

The channels of global crises contagion for banks include interbank lending, exposure through the various markets of instruments issued by other institutions, exposure through investments or loans to other non-home country entities and derivatives counterparty risk, second-order exposure through their borrowers (both corporate and retail) to any external shock, and all types of external shocks which could have an impact on the real local economy and global markets in which local players participate (e.g. commodities), among many others. Honohan (2008) notes that international credit-risk transfer has been a prominent feature of the past crisis with European financial institutions absorbing a sizable share of credit risk through their purchase of securitized mortgages.

4.4.2 Financial Contagion: Credit-Risk Transfer and Pure Contagion (Loss of Confidence and Changing Risk Aversion)

Financial contagion through credit-risk transfer is one channel whereby a crisis in one market could be transferred to a number of other markets. Reisen (2008) discusses the vanishing of the 'decoupling' myth, recounting that the fall in emerging market stocks, bonds and currencies proves that developed and emerging markets are linked. The IMF estimates that each one percentage point increase in a financial stress index (FSI) in advanced economies results in 0.3% increase in MENA countries FSI and up to 0.5% drop in GDP and markets are more integrated than previously thought.

The same argument is expandable to credit-risk transfer between developed markets, with financial innovation resulting in more integration rather than less, and in a more opaque manner given the complexity of the instruments. For Portugal, Italy, Greece and Spain (PIGS), the impact of the direct write-downs taken by banks and other non-bank financial institutions was only one aspect of the credit-risk transfer which took place in the last crisis. Worse, financial contagion through the shift in global-risk premiums and drying up of liquidity in international markets has affected these countries' ability to roll over their external funding and how much it will cost them to do so if they are able to refinance. In Chapter 3, I gave an example of how rising funding costs and drying up of liquidity impacted Greece and pushed it to the brink of default. But Greece does not have the worst metrics of its peers nor globally, according to the BIS, Italy's net debt stood at 97.4% in 2009, Japan had net debt of 96.5% and Greece comes in third at 86.1%. So in reality, as pointed out by Professor Niall Ferguson at the CFA Annual Conference, May 2010, 'PIGs 'R' US', the metrics of doom for developed countries all show excessive leverage and as such will react the same way to financial contagion, it is not just the PIGs.

Central and Eastern Europe, Middle East and Africa (CEMEA), and Central and Eastern Europe (CEE) have suffered the most through credit-risk transfer and by the foreign banks operating in these countries, and in some cases *dominating* the local banking sector, themselves taking write-downs. CEE countries were discussed in Chapter 3. I would like to focus on MENA countries here. MENA capital markets had major corrections in 2007 and 2008, losing around USD0.45 trillion in capitalization (41% of 2009e MENA GDP), albeit on the back of their own regional cycle, and stock market over valuation, but tipped over by the meltdown in the global markets which brought their collapse forward and increased its depth once the correction started.

Loss of confidence resulting from the current crisis was evident in what happened to Russia's foreign exchange reserves as individuals rushed to change local currency into foreign currency – this phenomenon of 'dollarization' is not just a by-product of financial contagion, but could signal a bigger problem where a country's nationals do not have confidence in the outlook of their country because of political or macroeconomic reasons. The key indicator to monitor is the level of foreign exchange reserves to banking sector liabilities (M2) in the case of a loss of confidence crisis. If reserves are below M2, individuals rush to convert domestic currency into foreign currency and lead to pressures on the currency, as was the case with Russia and indeed a number of markets pre a devaluation episode.

Figure 4.5 depicts the pattern of credit-risk transfer within and between global zones in the past crisis and the contagion cycle, highlighting how a crisis that starts with individual institutional failures can evolve into a systemic crisis.

4.4.3 Financial Contagion: Capital Flows

Capital flows are another channel whereby a crisis in one market could be transferred to other markets. Reinhart and Reinhart (2008) identify

Figure 4.5. Credit-Risk Transfer within and between Global Zones* and the Contagion Cycle.

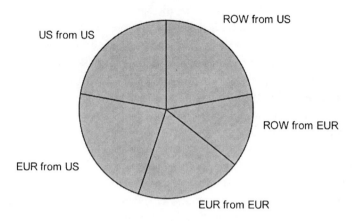

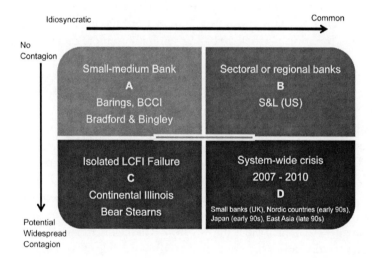

*Represents all credit-risk transferred globally from the US and Europe. Each slice represents intra or inter-regional transfers. Thus 'EUR from EUR' represents the credit-risk transferred from one European institution to another; 'ROW from US' represents credit risk emanating from the US and assumed by an institution in the rest of the world.
Source: Reisen, 2008 and adaptation of Hoggarth & Reidhill, 2003.

capital bonanzas in 181 countries during 1980–2007 and for a subset of 66 nations from 1960–2007. They contend that identifying these 'capital flow bonanzas' is a useful tool to understand the swings in investor interest in foreign markets as reflected in asset price booms and crashes, and for *predicting financial crises* and *sovereign defaults*. The authors identify two eras of booms over the past three decades: 1975 to 1982 and the current period from around 2000 to date. Given that the first wave in Latin American countries mostly ended in the emerging market debt crisis of the 1980s, this bodes ominously for the near term for countries with *high inflows from 2006 to 2008*. These include: industrial countries with house-price booms (for example Ireland, Spain, the UK and the US) and nations in Central and Eastern Europe (like Bulgaria, Romania and Slovenia) and MENA countries (both in North Africa and in the GCC, although the latter to a lesser extent). The authors find that about 61% of the countries who experience capital flow bonanzas have a *higher probability of banking crises* than countries which did not.

According to the Bank of England's June 2009 FSR, net purchases of domestic financial assets by foreigners in G20 countries increased significantly from 2000 to 2006 when it peaked at almost USD2.3 trillion. These purchases turned into total liquidations of around USD500 billion at the start of 2008, before rebounding again in 2008 to modest levels, a change of USD2.8 trillion. For emerging market economies, the liquidations amounted to almost USD150 billion in 2008, down from almost USD200 billion in purchases in 2007 – a hefty swing of USD350 billion – arguably a more significant drop for these smaller economies.

Capital flows to emerging markets could come in the form of long-term stable foreign direct investment (FDI) or short-term hot 'portfolio' investments, with the latter being one of the main causes of the Asian crisis in the late 1990s. In terms of FDI, the top 10 developing countries by magnitude of FDI inflows over the period from 2000 to 2007 received a total of USD1.3 trillion out of total FDI inflows to all developing countries of USD2.0 trillion over the same period. These countries included China, Russia, Brazil, Mexico, Turkey, India, Poland, Chile, Ukraine and Thailand (sub-total for Brazil, Russia, India and China (BRICs), was USD0.84 trillion, respectively). While in magnitude this seems small – given the trillions thrown around in the discussion of bank losses – this figure compared to the combined GDP of BRICs of USD6.9 trillion in 2007 is huge. Equity inflows to all developing countries booked almost 3% of their combined GDP in 2007 while outflows stood at circa 1% of GDP.

Similarly capital flows to the MENA region in the form of swings in FDI or portfolio investment, along with the reversal of the US carry trade, have had a significant impact. Cross-border flows between MENA and the rest of the world in 2007 ranged between 5% up to 10% of MENA GDP, up from 0.5% to 1% in 1999 and thus had become much more systemically significant. Capital flows to the region dropped to a mere USD1.9 trillion in 2008, from USD10.5 trillion in 2007.

Foreign exchange reserves, in addition to being affected by loss of confidence crises, are another potential channel of contagion from a flows perspective. As the USD constitutes anywhere from 50% to 70% of global foreign exchange reserves (estimated at USD7.5 trillion as of the end of 2008, of which China captures around USD2.0 trillion, followed by Japan at around USD1.0 trillion), volatility in the value of the USD vis-a-vis other currencies could result in large fluctuations in the value of these holdings. Furthermore, with increasing volatility in global currencies at large as the markets continue to absorb the implications of the new economic order, means reserves will also continue to be affected.

4.4.4 Foreign Trade: Monsoon Effect

Contagion could also occur through foreign trade channels. However, because it is grounded in the actual trade of physical goods, this channel could be considered the least harmful as it is also of a slow-burn nature. Nonetheless, in 2009–10 the IMF estimates global trade to have fallen by at least 12%. Using the current account balance as a percent of GDP as a proxy for foreign trade, HSBC and the EIU presented an interesting analysis of financial stress in selected countries. They also look at two other indicators for the impact of contagion, short-term debt as a percent of foreign exchange reserves and bank loan/deposit ratio to gauge the slack or lack thereof in countries' domestic financial systems. Based on this scheme, they classify South Africa, followed by Hungary, Poland, South Korea and Mexico as 'high-risk' countries in the case of contagion. In October 2008 Hungary did indeed secure a USD25 billion support package from the IMF and other multilateral institutions aimed at stemming growing capital outflows and related currency pressures. Mexico followed suit in April 2009, securing a USD47 billion credit line from the IMF. This analysis is presented in Figure 4.6.

This author disagrees with China's placement at the bottom of the list. In 2008 the US imported USD338 billion of goods from China – equivalent to 8% of China's GDP of USD4.4 trillion. With slowing global growth, emerging markets dependent on exports will have to change their business models.

For the MENA region, exports over the period (1999–2008) were 40% of regional GDP (non-oil exports 15%), the weakness in the dollar affected the region's current account negatively, given that 25% of the region's exports are in the form of oil, a commodity denominated in USD. A strengthening dollar would help improve this. On the other hand, MENA imports were at 32% of GDP over the period from 1999 to 2008 – with a weakening Euro, imports are cheaper and this would have a mild negative impact on the current account as increases in imports originating from Europe takes place.

Figure 4.6. Contagion Risk in Emerging Markets and Net Official Flows to Developing Countries (USD Billion).***

Country	Current Account % of GDP	Short-term Debt % of reserves	Bank's Loans/Deposits Ratio	Overall Risk Ranking
South Africa	-10.4	81	1.09	17
Hungary	-4.3	79	1.3	16
Poland	-8	38	1.03	14=
South Korea	1.3	102	1.3	14=
Mexico	-2.5	39	0.93	12=
Pakistan	-7.8	27	0.99	12=
Brazil	-1.5	22	1.36	10=
Turkey	-2.3	70	0.83	10=
Russia	1.5	28	1.51	9
Argentina	0.2	63	0.74	8
Venezuela	0.8	58	0.75	7
Indonesia	1.2	88	0.62	6
Thailand	0.3	17	0.88	5
India	-2.4	9	0.74	4
Taiwan	7.9	26	0.87	3
Malaysia	11.3	15	0.72	2
China	5.2	7	0.68	1

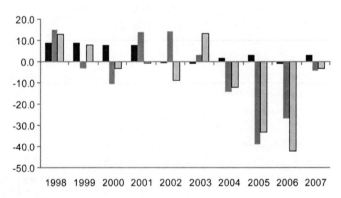

Sources: HSBC, EIU.
*2009 forecast. ** Higher score implies higher risk. *** GDF 2008, World Bank.

4.4.5 Outlook: Real Economy

The past crisis will have a huge impact on the global economy going forward, in line with the issues raised earlier with regards to business models of banks and industrial firms, financial and non-financial agents, regulation, government finance and so on. This impact will unravel with sizable global output losses, a credit crunch, deleveraging of the global economy, more bankruptcies in industries, commercial real estate losses, contagion to other developed and to emerging markets, and indeed consumer bankruptcies as well. This section discusses briefly the credit crunch hypothesis and deleveraging; lower global output; demand side rebalancing and Chimerica; and equity and housing markets.

4.4.6 Credit Crunch Hypothesis and Deleveraging the Global Economy

Demirgüç-Kunt and Detragiache (2005) put forward a credit crunch hypothesis which has found strong empirical support in Lindgren et al (1996), Kaminsky and Reinhart (1999) and Eichengreen and Rose (1998). They postulate that markets are 'starved' for credit following a crisis which results in output losses and bankruptcies of less well capitalized entities. Dell'Ariccia et al (2006) also give strong support to a credit crunch hypothesis following downturns and that banking crises do have a strong impact on the performance of the real economy. They find that more financially dependent sectors suffer more than other sectors during crises; furthermore the magnitude of the effect is sizable. More financially dependent sectors lose about 1% of growth in each crisis year compared to less financially dependent sectors, with the effects more pronounced in developing countries, in countries where the private sector has less access to foreign finance and where the crises are more severe. I would also add to this list markets with poorly developed bond markets, as their only source of financing would be banks.

Another study by Demirgüç-Kunt, Detragiache and Gupta in 2000 uses aggregate and bank-level data for several countries to study the aftermath of a banking crises and finds that growth of both deposits and credit slows down substantially with recovery beginning in the second year after the crisis and is not led by a resumption in credit growth. Banks, including the stronger ones, reallocated their asset portfolio away from loans, and this seems to be applicable to the current crisis. During periods of market turmoil, banks tend to shift their portfolio allocation towards cash instruments and reserves rather than the traditional extension of credit and other products to the market. This can be illustrated by the sharp drop in the ratio of interbank lending to total bank reserves in the US and the drastic fall in loan multiplier (loans to reserves, as opposed to the traditional money multiplier which is the reciprocal of the reserve ratio – loan to reserves is a more accurate metric to gauge lending activity progression) over the period from January 1999, through to May 2009 as shown by Figure 4.7.

Figure 4.7. US Ratio of Interbank Lending to Total Bank Reserves (Loan Supply and Loan Multiplier).

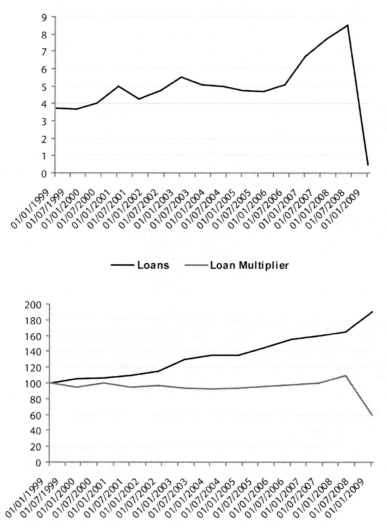

Sources: Federal Reserve Bank of St. Louis, LBS WAC Presentation, Thursday 24 September, 2009.

4.4.7 Lower Potential Output

As a result of the financial crisis, the IMF has forecast global output over the 2008–10 period will potentially be USD10.2 trillion lower than what it would have been had the crisis not occurred. To put this figure in perspective, and although it is the forecast for losses over a three-year period, total global GDP in 2008 was USD67.1 trillion.

4.4.8 Demand Side Rebalancing and Chimerica

China and some other economies which have had export-led growth strategies and have run current account surpluses will have to try and find alternative drivers of demand for their products, either in the form of tapping new markets, which are highly populated and have not yet seen a boom in consumption, or by propelling domestic demand. This should help offset lower demand by economies such as the UK, US and part of the Eurozone, which have traditionally run large current account deficits. Taking China as an example, is this shift feasible? Can the Chinese be turned into a nation of consumers instead of savers? So far, to combat the impact of the global recession on its economy, China has increased its fiscal stimulus significantly; this stimulus goes to fund centrally planned projects, mainly in construction and infrastructure. True China is a vast nation, but how long can it build bridges in rural areas or in some cases 'ghost' towns. This stimulus and credit expansion have both resulted in a real estate bubble developing in China and overheating of the stock market, what are the implications when these imbalances are rectified, not only for China but for the US?

China has some USD2.4 trillion of foreign exchange reserves of which a large allocation is made to US government bonds and as such has been financing by its savings overspending in the US which is 20 times as rich on a per capita GDP basis. Moreover, the structure of US debt is skewed towards the short term, which renders it even more vulnerable to changes in China's economic well being.

Another imbalance that has created significant tension is in the Eurozone, with the impending Greek default stretching at the seams of a loosely knit union of diverse nations with different languages. Germany and France, net exporters and fiscally strong, are having to pay for the excesses in Greece. A large part of Greek government expenditure goes towards generous pension payments, almost double their German counterparts. Finally, the state of the world economy with OECD countries which have only 18% of the world's population, capturing 75% of its total GDP and given the ageing and longevity problems faced by these countries, is also a major global imbalance, albeit a slow-bleed one, which will continue to rectify over the medium to long runs, or will otherwise result in significant geopolitical tensions.

4.4.9 Deleveraging, Slow Job Growth Ahead and Real Estate Bubble Bursts

Extending the argument presented in Chapter 1, firms are still going bankrupt at a high rate and deleveraging is only starting, which will have significant implications on the real economy in terms of employment levels and output.

Consumers in developed and some developing markets are also highly leveraged, 'households [were] consuming the present value of their future wealth, which they [did] not actually possess in the first place', as the governor of the Central Bank of Turkey, Mr Yilmaz, announced on 20 May 2010, which means that they too will have to deleverage – so this looks a great deal worse than the balance sheet recession of Japan in the 1990s, as not only corporate are highly leveraged, but also consumers.

What are the characteristics of a balance sheet recession? Richard Koo's *The Holy Grail of Macroeconomics: Lessons from Japan's Great Recession*, identifies a 'Yin –Yang', 'Shadow – Light' cycle of bubbles and balance sheet recessions. In 'Yin' or shadow or dark part of the bubble cycle, a bubble exists, monetary policy is tightened pushing the bubble to collapse, asset prices fall excessively leaving the private sector with too much debt compared to assets, forcing it to minimize its debts. This results in the economy falling in a balance sheet recession. As agents start paying down debt, monetary policy stops functioning as no matter how low rates go, loan demand does not respond, the money multiplier is negative, and fiscal policy becomes the core economic tool to sustain demand. In time, the private sector finishes bringing down its debt, ending the balance sheet recession, but still is 'scared' to borrow even at low rates. In the 'Yang' or 'light' part of the bubble cycle, private sector gradually forgets its fear of borrowing, monetary policy starts working again. The use of fiscal policy becomes a burden crowding out private sector investments, so the focus shifts on reducing the budget deficit. The economy becomes healthy again, the private sector slips into over confidence and another bubble starts to evolve. During Japan's balance sheet recession which started in the early 1990s, cumulative losses on shares and land up till 2008 booked USD15 trillion, or three times Japan's GDP.

4.4.10 Real Estate Structural Issues

As a real estate bubble was at the root of this crisis and given that real estate affordability indicators in many OECD countries are unfavourable, and as commercial real estate continues to be held on bank books without the sizable haircuts the last cycle warranted, I believe that there is still a significant real estate overhang to be worked out through the cycle over the coming few years. Taking Japan as an example, commercial real estate prices in the late 1990s had fallen by a hefty 87% from their peak levels a decade earlier.

Turning to indicators of house price evolution and affordability, there are three key indicator sets of price evolution: house price appreciation year-on-year, house price-to-disposable income ratios and house price-to-rent ratios. Using 1992 as the base year with an index value of 100, there are four OECD countries which have seen drops in house prices in real and nominal terms: Japan, Germany, Switzerland and Korea. At the other end of the spectrum Ireland for example has risen the most, at 436% in nominal terms and 233% in real terms. The bigger the bubble, the more financial pain there is when it bursts, we have seen this in the case of Irish banks, where loans to the real estate sector booked a sizable 60% of GNP. The Irish government in addition to guaranteeing the deposits and most bonds of Irish banks, has committed to spend, around €40 billion on a National Asset Management Agency to buy non-performing development loans from banks, and to invest around 30 billion euros in Irish banks. Despite this large injection (equivalent to half of GNP), the outlook for Irish banks remains bleak, according to Professor Morgan Kelly.

Just looking at house price appreciation, if we consider economies which saw house prices rise by more than 200% as having experienced a bubble, then Australia, the UK, Denmark, New Zealand, Spain, Norway, the Netherlands and Ireland all did.

Another measure of affordability is house-prices to rent, compared to a long-term average of 100. Reasonably interpreted as similar in concept to a price-earnings multiple for a company, it is the value of a house compared to the average annual rent. The higher the multiple or the greater the deviation from 100, the more expensive houses are; the lower the multiple than the 100 threshold, the more affordable houses are. Thus for the countries which saw drops in house prices in 2007, this affordability indicator improved: Japan had a ratio of 70.3%, Germany 72.4%, Switzerland 85.1% and Korea 109.7% in 2007, compared to 128.4%, 93.8%, 107%, and 113% respectively in 1992.

4.4.11 Recent Housing Market Performance

Out of 19 developed countries surveyed by the *Economist*, house prices in 2007 saw drops in the US, Japan, Ireland and Germany. In 2008, the number of countries witnessing drops in housing prices rose to 16. However, out of this sample, only Japan and Hong Kong have seen drops in housing prices over the period from 1997 to 2008 while the rest continue to have accumulated significant rises. This goes against the IMF's World Economic Outlook of 2003 estimated five-year duration of housing bubbles (costing around 8% of GDP), indicating that the housing cycle is rather a 10-year one.

To put the drop in the recent house prices in perspective, for the first time in US history household net worth has declined because of housing price drops (in the 2000 recession household net worth dropped because of the fall in equity prices). In the 1990s, despite the savings and loans crisis, household net worth growth had only slowed, but not dropped in absolute terms.

4.4.12 UK Housing Market

A pessimistic report by Numis Securities has estimated that house prices in Britain could fall by a further 40% to 55% from current levels, despite having witnessed a 17.6% drop in 2008. To put the exposure to the housing market in perspective, UK banks had around GBP400 billion exposure in the form of securitized household loans, a significant exposure. Given their systemic significance, the UK is especially susceptible to deterioration in household net worth and property prices.

On the micro level, the market has been seeing deal flow of commercial real estate on the back of the crisis. In 2009, this included a 700 million commercial real estate portfolio sold by Aviva Investors, one of the largest property investment funds in the UK and more recently in 2010 after he went bankrupt, the Simon Halabi portfolio estimated at GBP3 billion and including some iconic buildings was put up for sale. The problem is while some transactions are being made, a lot of banks are still carrying on their books huge inventories priced at pre-crisis levels. One example is the Lloyds portfolio, which is burdened by all the real estate assets inherited from HBOS.

4.4.13 Capital Markets Structural Issues: The Impact of the Crisis

The turmoil in these markets and their dismal performance shows the extent of global wealth destruction. In 2008, USD30 trillion, or 42% of global GDP, was wiped off the capitalization of global *equity markets*, far exceeding the estimate by the IMF of the cost of equity market bubbles at around 4% of GDP (with the bust lasting for around two and a half years). Equity capital markets rebounded in 2009, however, by around 40%, with some markets in the BRICs region, such as Brazil, witnessing increases close to 100%. In countries such as Iceland, the equity market collapsed to just 20% of GDP, down from 120% of GDP.

To gauge the impact of the crisis on market structure and sustainability of certain capital market trends, I turn to look at a set of capital market indicators *pre-crisis*, subdivided into four main sets. The first set is equity market capitalization to GDP, which shows how developed equity capital markets are in terms of the value of listed corporate to GDP. The second is debt market capitalization to GDP, to see how big debt capital markets are compared to GDP; the larger debt capital markets, the more sources of funding corporates have and the more diversified the financial sector is as less risk is undertaken by banks in the form of traditional lending. The third is the level of share prices compared to earnings; how many times current market prices are the estimated earnings of corporates. The fourth is dividend yields, which indicate the returns an investor receives from dividends on holding stocks in the market.

In 2007 equity market cap to GDP for OECD countries ranged from a low of 71% in New Zealand to a high of 480% in Switzerland. Figure 4.8 (first panel) illustrates this. Economic theory is silent on how big equity capital markets should be compared to GDP, however, at large, given expected lower levels of leverage across the board, it is most likely that market size compared to GDP will shrink.

For debt capital markets in 2007, this ranged from 5% on the low end for Mexico to 234% in Japan and the US. Again economic theory is silent with regards to the optimal levels of market cap to GDP of each individual market and indeed the ratio of the size of debt capital markets to equity capital markets. In some countries the latter is one to one, in others, debt capital markets are twice the size of equity markets, depending on their stage of development. Given that the crisis has directly hit debt capital markets and mortgage securities in specific, the size of debt capital markets to GDP should also shrink.

Price-to-earnings ratio gives an indication of how expensive a market is relative to the underlying earnings generated by the companies listed. In 2007, the US had a 46x PER, indicating it would take an investor on average 46 years of earnings to recoup the price paid to buy the stocks. Greece, Portugal and Japan were trading at 28 times and the UK and Ireland at a reasonable 12 and 10 respectively. Clearly ratios in excess of 20 should raise alarm bells from a practitioner's perspective as to whether a bubble is in the making. Figure 4.8 (last panel) illustrates P/E ratios for selected countries. Putting the past crisis in perspective, high price to earnings ratios are an indicator of bubbles developing. Given that corporate earnings, at least the proportion attributable to listed financials institutions which are a large part of all major equity market indices, are going to be structurally lower in the future because of the shift in business model to using less leverage, we should see market price/earnings ratios fall. This is contingent, of course, on the financial sector not being able to 'discover' new sources of earnings. Manufacturing industries as well, with lower debt levels for consumers, will likely feel the squeeze.

In terms of dividend yields, Ireland topped the list, providing yields of 17%, the UK 1.0% and the US 1.9%. Much research in corporate finance has been dedicated to dividend theory, starting with Miller and Modigliani's capital structure theory, I, II and III, to modern-day literature. The argument hinges on investors being indifferent to getting higher dividends or more price appreciation if the tax rates are the same on both types of gains and any returns of projects the company they have invested in undertakes are greater than their required return. This does not seem to be applied by corporates when determining 'optimal' dividend levels. Dividends, however, could be taken as

Figure 4.8. Key Capital Market Indicators for Selected OECD Countries (2007).

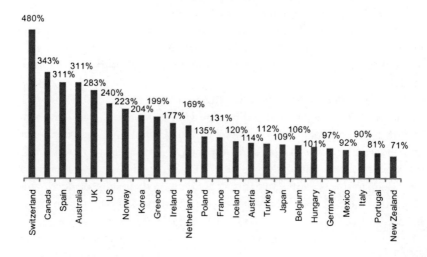

Equity Market Capitalization/GDP

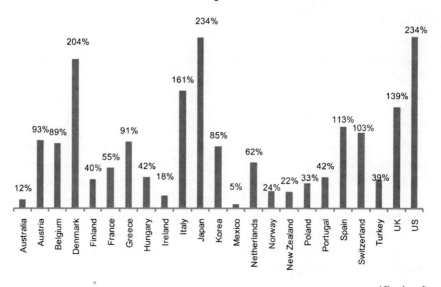

Debt Market Capitalization/GDP

(*Continued*)

Figure 4.8. Continued.

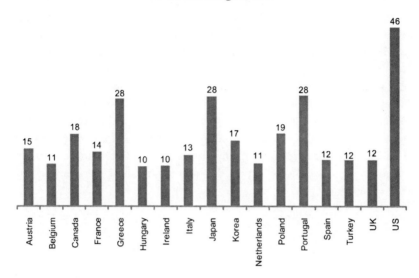

Price Earnings Ratio

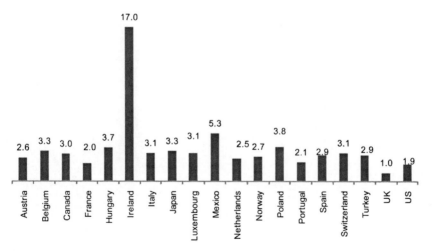

Dividend Yields

Source: Graphs 1 and 2: OECD, author's calculations. Graphs 3 and 4: World Federation of Exchanges, author's calculations.

a proxy for corporate health: companies only distribute dividends when they have excess funds or free cash flows to shareholders. Since dividends tend to be sticky, management is reluctant to change them, because once changed, it's very difficult to go back to lower levels. The reason being also the signalling component in dividends, that is if a company increases its dividends it is signalling to the market that it is expecting to do better in future, not just that it has done well in the past. So it cannot go back and decrease its dividends, as this would indicate it believes it will do worse going forward. Literature on information asymmetries and corporate actions, however, would argue that the picture is more muddled by lemons trying to signal to the market that they are not. For the financial sector, given that the outlook for regulation is still unclear, and for corporates facing less ability to fund their business needs through leverage, we should expect drops in dividends as these entities boost their capitalization.

Chapter 5

REGULATORY REGIMES AND
RESPONSE TO THE CRISIS

José Viñals, IMF Financial Counsellor and Director, Monetary and Capital Markets Department, says *Regulatory Reform in Difficult Times, [is] A Tough Balancing Act.* In his talk in Berlin on 20 May 2010 on effective financial market regulation, he outlines five key areas where a delicate balance needs to be struck in the redesign of regulatory frameworks: macroprudential and micro-prudential dimensions; regulation and supervision; banks and non-banks; safety of the system versus its efficiency; and regulations which are tailored to national requirements, without compromising consistency with international regulation, versus international regulation. 'Over the years, banks, investment banks, savings institutions, and insurance companies...had all gotten into one another's businesses,' says Paulson. 'The products they designed and sold had become infinitely more complex, and big financial institutions had become inextricably intertwined, *stitched tightly together by complex credit* arrangements' (emphasis added). And he goes on to explain how the regulatory structure [in the US] had not kept up with the changes in the financial markets and as a result the country had a 'patchwork' system, the same pattern repeated in other major financial centres.

In my view, this will always be the regulators' dilemma: the delicate balance of regulating markets when markets will always be faster, leaner and meaner than regulators. After all they are in the business of making money and they don't like rules. They hire the high flyers (regulators usually attract more docile types) and are evaluated on the basis of how much money they make, whatever the form of that evaluation is. This outlook is also shared by Bill Gross, managing director at PIMCO investors, as Mohamed El Erian, PIMCO's CEO explains in his book *When Markets Collide.* In one of the investment outlook reports put out by Gross, he says, 'The modern financial complex has morphed into something unrecognizable to many astute market veterans and academics'. *This again reinforces the concept of the sector being too big to FRAME, fail, regulate, audit, manage, evaluate and also in the literal sense frame in terms of being fully comprehended by academics, regulators and practitioners.*

The past and ongoing crisis has brought this eternal regulator dilemma to a new height, and the question of which regulatory regimes were the most effective or minimized losses during the downturn: how they reacted to the past crisis, the actions taken, the set of policy tools and the impact of these on losses realized and on the speed of crisis unravelling and its resolution. The debate will shape the face of financial regulation over the coming decades and the pendulum will swing between both ends of the spectrum of 'light touch' and 'iron shackle' regulation until a balance is found. This chapter is structured as follows: in the first section the architecture of the existing regulatory regimes pre-crisis are outlined, section two highlights the losses by type of regulatory regime, section three discusses the various policy responses and tools on a country and global level and section four highlights planned policy changes triggered by the crisis.

5.1 Existing Regulatory Regimes Pre-Crisis

Nier (2009) reviews financial stability and regulatory frameworks architecture and the costs and benefits associated thereof, in light of the recent crisis. He weighs the strengths and weaknesses of existing structures including the integrated model, the twin peaks model and hybrid models.. The single-integrated regulator (SIR) model has one regulator overseeing market regulation (commercial banks, mutual funds and pension funds and insurance companies) and the central bank overseeing lender of last resort (LOLR) activities and payments oversight. Examples of SIR-type models are the UK (before June 2010), Denmark, Norway, Sweden and Switzerland, among others. Twin peaks models have the central bank overseeing systemic risk, including LOLR and payment systems and all potentially systemic institutions and another regulatory body handling regulation of financial services. Examples of TP-type systems include the Netherlands, Bulgaria and South Africa, France, Italy, Portugal and Spain.

5.2 Losses by Type of Regulatory Regime

In some preliminary empirical results covering the period from 2Q07 to 2Q08, Nier (2009) classifies the losses associated with each main type of regulatory regime (single-integrated regulator, SIR versus twin peaks, TP) in Europe and finds greater losses associated with the SIR model. While total losses in TP countries booked around USD40 billion, the comparative figure for SIR countries is USD126 billion. Figure 5.1 shows the tally of losses by type of regulatory regime in a number of countries. The overall loss to credit ratio also draws a similar picture with the total for TPs at 0.5%, compared to SIRs

Figure 5.1. Bank Losses and Losses to Credit Ratios for SIRs vs TP Regulatory Systems.

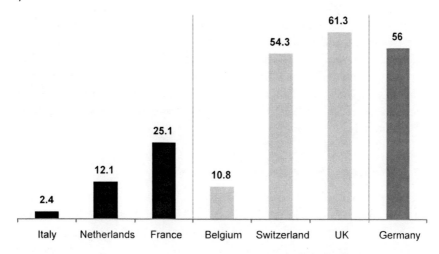

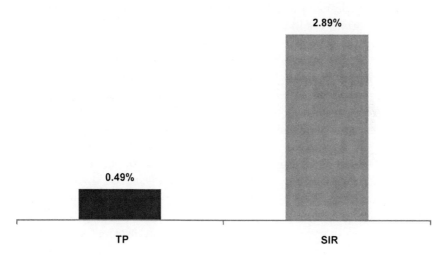

Source: Nier, 2009.

at 2.9%. These findings support the argument that having a twin peaks-type regulatory setup is more effective. With a SIR such as the UK (before June 2010), there is potential for a lot of 'lost' information in having the Bank of England only regulating LOLR activities as it is relatively detached from the banking supervisory function and all the information bank supervisors are privy to, including regular discussions with market players. Therefore, twin peaks systems have been found to be more effective.

5.3 Policy Response

Regulatory policy response to the crisis has been far-reaching, from direct intervention in the financial sector through capital injections, purchase of assets, central bank provision of liquidity and guarantees, in addition to traditional coordinated monetary action and fiscal stimulus. Governments used all the weapons in their artillery to combat the crisis, as well as measures which have not been used anytime in near history such as quantitative easing. These measures have collectively ranged from less than 1% of GDP to almost 20% in the UK.

5.3.1 Domestic Policy Responses Overview

In 2008 the IMF's GFSR identified three interrelated areas that authorities need to continue to address as the global financial system deleverages: a) insufficient capital, b) falling and uncertain asset valuations and (c) dysfunctional capital markets. This is quite a challenge given that monetary policy was virtually neutralized, not only because of some of the characteristics of balance sheet recessions which were applicable, but more importantly, because rates are at very low levels and as such transmission channels were partly severed. The latter occurred on the back of counterparty risk in the interbank market, increasing importance of the 'shadow' banking system, the more extensive use of wholesale funding markets as opposed to deposits – which are more directly linked to regulatory reserve requirements and base rates – and the movement away from a stable deposit base to larger proportion of short-term funding by banks through wholesale funding markets. Governments have responded as such by directly pumping liquidity into their banking systems in the form of capital, thereby part or fully nationalizing failed institutions; providing asset protection, liquidity extension and guarantees to banks and instruments issued by banks; and attempting to enhance transparency in financial markets and kick start the securitization markets using various tools. A lot of these actions have been discussed in details in Chapters 3 and 4 and I now turn to addressing the policy tools not discussed previously.

5.3.2 Monetary Policy and Quantitative Easing

With the onset of the crisis, policy makers fell back on the traditional monetary policy tool: slashing interest rates. The dramatic evolution of interest rate cuts to almost zero percent in developed economies and the degree of coordination during the implementation between the various authorities since 2007 was unprecedented. Having exhausted this tool, and with the disconnect between base rates and interbank and other market rates – because of the shift in risk premiums (in general investors discovered they had been underpricing risk across the board), which at one point resulted in the London Interbank Offer Rate (LIBOR) spreads hiking to as high as 360 bps in April 2009 up from an average spread of a few basis points to base rates prior to the crisis (banks were seen as having credit risk higher than previously thought, after all they can *fail*) – it was clear that central banks had to resort to new tools. The Fed announced USD1.2 trillion in March 2009 in quantitative easing and the Bank of England GBP75 billion, respectively – the latter was raised to GBP175 billion subsequently. A number of other not-so-mainstream liquidity-creating tools were used such as asset swaps. Collectively these led to the growth of the Fed's balance sheet by more than 250% and the Bank of England's balance sheet by more than 220% from March 2007 to date.

What has the effect of quantitative easing been? The debate is still ongoing between policy makers, and it is still difficult to judge with aftershocks of the crisis and tumbleweed continuing to blow. Figure 5.2 highlights key policy rate changes and central bank balance sheet expansion in the US, the UK and Europe. The ECB's balance sheet growth, while more moderate than the Fed's and the Bank of England's, was still sizable.

5.3.3 Fiscal Stimulus, Growing Budget Deficits and Debt Issuance

Fiscal stimulus in G-20 countries in 2009 was projected to be around 1.5% of GDP according to the IMF, while overall fiscal balance in advanced economies was projected to deteriorate by 3.25% to −7% percent of GDP in 2009. The US has announced a stimulus package to the tune of 2% of GDP in 2009 and for a total of 4.6% until 2011 (or USD787 billion). Figure 5.3 details headline support as a percentage of GDP for a number of countries, and the allocation by type of policy tool used.

While some countries had a better fiscal standing at the beginning of the crisis, others did not. Canada, China, France, Germany, the UK and the US had smaller levels of deficits, public debt and interest rates. Others, like India and Italy, had higher real interest rates and debt levels. Japan had the highest level of debt among developed countries, standing at almost 200% of GDP. The size of the increase in public debt, however, was largest for the UK and the US, for the former increasing by half the amount outstanding and by a third almost for the US. Figure 5.4 compares crisis stimulus packages, budget balance, public debt levels and policy measures by large developed countries.

Figure 5.2. Policy Rates and Central Banks Balance Sheet Expansion.

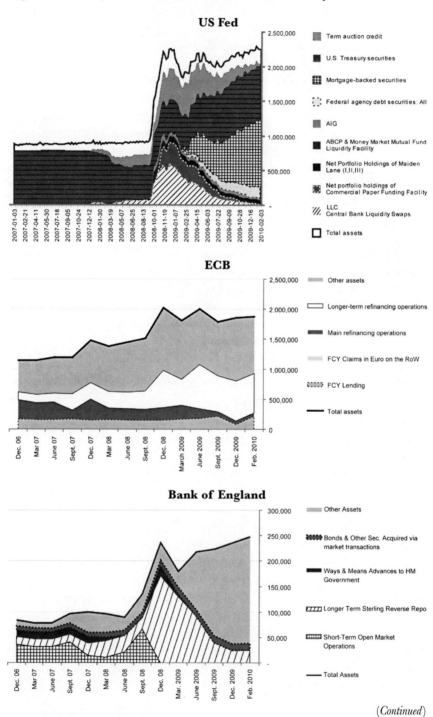

(*Continued*)

Figure 5.2. Continued.

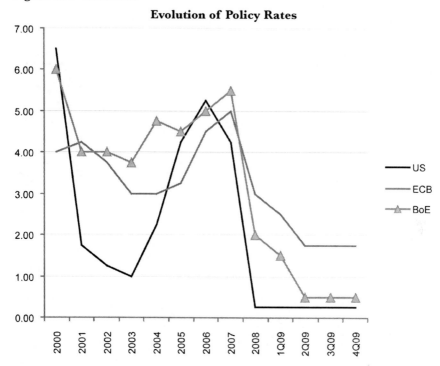

Evolution of Policy Rates

Sources: Federal Reserve, ECB, BoE.

5.3.3a Increase in Debt and Crowding Out

The increase in government debt is also forecast to have significant crowding-out effects: for every 10% of increase in government debt, global GDP is forecast to drop by 1.3% (1.2% for the US, respectively). Furthermore, fiscal deterioration in advanced economies poses an additional threat to future global growth, as these very same nations have to deal with the effects of a rapidly ageing population and the consequences on pension funding deficits, among others. The first nation to show serious threats to its fiscal position was Greece in October 2009 which has a forecast public debt to GDP for 2010 of 120%, with concerns about the fiscal stability of Portugal (90% of GDP), Spain (68% of GDP) and Italy (130% of GDP).

5.3.4 Policy Response to Contagion Threats to Emerging Markets

Thus far the IMF has pledged USD1.1 trillion to help developing countries weather the crisis. From November 2008 to March 2009, the IMF has extended assistance to Romania, Ukraine, Hungary, Pakistan, Belarus, Latvia,

Figure 5.3. Headline Support for the Financial Sector and Upfront Financing Need (% of GDP).

	Capital Injection	Purchase of Assets/Lending by Treasury	Central Bank Support	Liquidity Provision & Other Central Bank Support	Guarantees	Total	Upfront Government Financing
North America							
Canada	0.0	8.8	0.0	1.6	11.7	22.1	8.8
US	4.0	6.0	1.1	31.3	31.3	73.7	6.3
Advance Europe							
Austria	5.3	0.0	0.0	0.0	30.0	35.3	5.3
Belgium	4.7	0.0	0.0	0.0	26.2	30.9	4.7
France	1.2	1.3	0.0	0.0	16.4	18.9	1.5
Germany	3.7	0.4	0.0	0.0	17.6	21.7	3.7
Greece	2.1	3.3	0.0	0.0	6.2	11.6	5.4
Ireland	5.3	0.0	0.0	0.0	257.0	262.3	5.3
Italy	1.3	0.0	0.0	2.5	0.0	3.8	1.3
Netherlands	3.4	2.8	0.0	0.0	33.7	39.9	6.2
Norway	0.0	13.8	0.0	0.0	0.0	13.8	13.8
Portugal	2.4	0.0	0.0	0.0	12.0	14.4	2.4
Spain	0.0	4.6	0.0	0.0	18.3	22.9	4.6
Sweden	2.1	5.3	0.0	15.3	47.3	70.0	5.8
Switzerland	1.1	0.0	0.0	10.9	0.0	12.0	1.1
UK	3.5	13.8	12.9	0.0	17.4	47.6	19.8
Asia Pacific							
Australia	0.0	0.7	0.0	0.0		0.7	0.7
Japan	2.4	6.7	0.0	0.0	3.9	13.0	0.2
Korea	2.5	1.2	0.0	0.0	10.6	14.3	14.3
Emerging Economies							
Argentina	0.0	0.9	0.0	0.0	0.0	0.9	0.0
Brazil	0.0	0.0	0.0	1.5	0.0	1.5	0.0
China	0.5	0.0	0.0	0.0	0.0	0.5	0.0
India	0.0	0.0	0.0	5.6	0.0	5.6	0.0
Indonesia	0.0	0.0	0.0	0.0	0.1	0.1	0.1
Hungary	1.1	0.0	0.0	4.0	1.1	6.2	1.1
Poland	0.4	0.0	0.0	0.0	3.2	3.6	0.4
Russia	0.1	0.4	2.9	3.2	0.5	7.1	0.6
Saudi Arabia	0.6	0.6	0.0	8.2		9.4	1.2
Turkey	0.0	0.0	0.0	0.2	0.0	0.2	0.0

Source: IMF.

Figure 5.4. Crisis Stimulus Packages, Budget Balance, Public Debt and Policy Measures by Large Countries.

Stimulus Packages in Large Countries

% of GDP	2008	2009	2010	Total
Canada	0	1.5	1.3	2.8
China	0.4	2	2	4.4
France	0	0.7	0.7	1.4
Germany	0	1.5	2	3.5
India	0	0.5		0.5
Italy	0	0.2	0.1	0.3
Japan	0.4	1.4	0.4	2.2
UK	0.2	1.4	-0.1	1.5
US	1.1	2	1.8	4.9
Average	0.5	1.6	1.3	3.4

(Continued)

Figure 5.4. Continued.

Change in over-all Budget Balance % of GDP

Relative to pre-crisis year	2008	2009	2010	Avg.
Canada	-0.9	-2.9	-3.2	-2.4
China	-1.1	-3.0	-3.0	-2.3
France	-0.6	-2.8	-3.6	-2.3
Germany		-3.2	-4.4	-3.8
India	-2.6	-3.3	-2.2	-2.7
Italy	-1.1	-2.4	-2.8	-2.1
Japan	-1.3	-3.7	-3.7	-2.9
UK	-1.5	-4.6	-5.4	-3.8
US	-3.5	-5.7	-6.1	-5.1
Average	**-2.0**	**-4.1**	**-4.4**	**-3.6**

Fiscal Balance & Public Debt Projections 2009

% of GDP	Overall Balance		Public debt	
	Pre-Crisis	Current	Pre-Crisis	Current
Canada	0.8	-1.5	61.0	63.0
China	-0.9	-2.0	13.4	22.2
France	-2.5	-5.5	63.0	72.3
Germany	-0.5	-3.3	61.1	76.1
India	-5.0	-8.5	69.8	82.7
Italy	-2.3	-3.9	104.1	109.4
Japan	-3.7	-7.1	194.2	217.0
UK	-2.1	-7.2	42.9	58.2
US	-3.2	-8.5	63.4	81.2

Measure	Canada	China	France	Germany	India	Italy	Japan	UK	US
Expenditure									
Infrastructure Investment	T	T	T	T	T		T	S	T
Support to SMEs &/or farmers				T			T		
Safety nets	T	T	T	T		T	T	T	T
Housing/construction support	T	T	T	T			T	T	
Strategic industries support	T	T		T	T				
Increase in public wage bill									
other	T	T	T	T	T		T	T	T
Revenue									
CIT/depreciation incentives	P		P				P		P
PIT/ exemptions deductions	P		P				P	P	P
Indirect tax reductions/exemptions		P	T	P	T			S	
Other							P	P	

Source: IMF. Measures announced as of 13 February, 2009. T: temporary measures (with explicit sunset provisions or time-bound spending S: self-reversing measures (costs are recouped by compensatory measures in the future ten years) P: permanent measures (with recurrent fiscal costs).

Iceland, Georgia, Armenia and Serbia of more than USD60 billion, ranging from 1% to 11% of GDP for these countries. The Institute of International Finance (IIF) has estimated that capital flows to emerging economies in 2009 will be 80% lower than in 2007. Thus the last G20 meeting in April 2009 in London saw global leaders pledging some USD500 billion to USD750 billion in additional resources for the IMF. The IMF has also introduced a new instrument, a Flexible Credit Line (FCL). This instrument is in effect a contingent line of credit and the first one has been requested by Mexico for USD47 billion. Details on other uses of the FCL to date are outlined in Appendix 1 and in earlier chapters.

Will this be enough to combat the consequences of the global credit crisis, the current credit crunch and the higher costs of capital to compensate for higher risk? During the boom cycle, development loans provided by international finance institutions, multi-lateral and regional development banks were crowded out by private sector lending and better access to international capital markets by member countries, especially middle-income countries. Net official lending has declined by as much as USD185 billion from 2003 to 2007 while the total loanable funds at the IMF stood at USD209.5 billion, of which only USD16.1 billion had been outstanding as of the end of 2008. Development institutions collectively suffered significant losses from prepayments by these countries, especially on one type of product which had been popular more than a decade earlier: variable rate loans (VLRs). This product was based on charging clients (countries) with a variable interest rate through a pass-through pool based on the average cost of funding of that pool. Given that most of these pools had been funded at a time when interest rates were significantly higher, the pursuant drop in interest rates triggered several prepayments and losses in interest income for these multilateral development institutions. As recently stated by a World Bank official not wishing to be quoted, these institutions are moving from a stage of 'excess capacity to lack of capacity thereof'.

5.4 Regulatory Challenges and Proposed Changes

The IMF identified a set of policy challenges ahead that would require addressing. These include policies to a) secure a backdrop for economic recovery, b) strengthen the banking sector and promote resumption of lending, c) revive securitization markets, d) prevent crises in emerging markets in Europe which remain vulnerable to deleveraging, e) ensure orderly disengagement or exit strategies for regulators, and f) to manage the recent transfer of private risks to sovereign balance sheets. It proposes the following priorities for reform: i) restoring market discipline, ii) addressing fiscal risks caused by financial institutions (the idea of a 'systemic tax'),

iii) living wills, iv) a macroprudential approach to policy making and v) integrating the oversight of LCFI's into the global financial market. Why is the road map for regulation in the near term so problematic and ultimately challenging? Also, if the regulator's list of priorities and 'to-do's is as long as the preceding one, ten key target areas – where do we start in order to fix the world and what are the delicate balances and trade-offs in the design of the global regulatory framework?

5.4.1 Banking Sectors and Individual Institutions are Too Big to FRAME: Fail, Too Big to Regulate, Too Big to Audit, Too Big to Manage, Too Big to Evaluate

The concept of too big to FRAME has been presented earlier in the book. The current size of the banking sectors in a number of countries and the size of selected banks relative to the GDP of their host countries is illustrated in Figure 5.5. *Bank assets to GDP range from 100% in the US to more than 800% in Switzerland.* Banks should support economic growth rather than economic growth supporting bank growth which seems to have been the case here given these size comparisons.

Moreover, the ratio of a single bank's assets to a host country's GDP should not be greater than a moderate proportion of its national GDP, deemed

Figure 5.5. Assets to GDP of Host Country and Selected Banks – Too Big to FRAME?

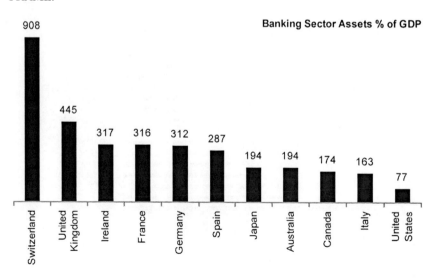

Figure 5.5. Continued.

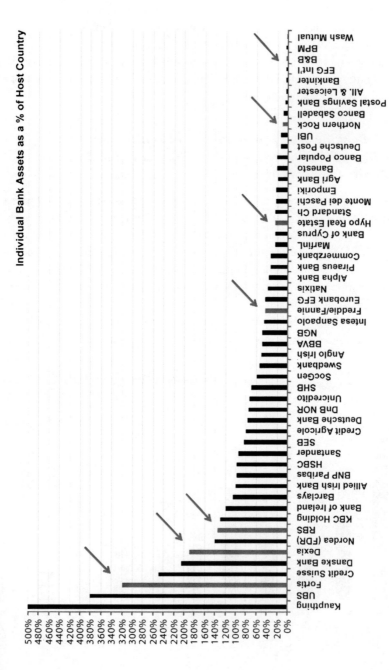

Source: Above: Bank of England FSR, June 2009; below: Citi Investment Research, updated by author; institutions in red received some form of government bailout.

reasonable to ensure a fairly diversified, non-concentrated sector in any given country. These ratios of more than 500% in the case of Icelandic Bank Kauphthing, Credit Suisse 250%, Dexia 200%, etc. explain why when two of these banks collapsed, they had to be rescued not by their hosts, but by cross-border coordinated efforts, in a sporadic manner. The case of financial centres is even more complicated and different rules will have to apply with the caveat being always how to safeguard the national system in the case of the unwinding or failure of any or a number of the international institutions operating in the host country or financial hub, examples are Switzerland as mentioned above with banking assets being 8x GDP and Bahrain, with banking assets at 11x GDP.

5.4.2 Turf Wars and Power Struggles

If indeed banking sectors have become too large for single countries to manage – how do we draw a map of future global regulation? This will definitely entail a lot of turf wars and power struggles, and if national regulators were difficult to manage in this respect, how could 'super' or 'supra' national regulators be?

5.4.3 Regulatory Overhaul and Sector Stability

Many countries have now, on the national level, undertaken overhauls of their regulatory arrangements: The UK has abolished the FSA and transferred its mandate to the Bank of England in June 2010; Germany has recently abolished BaFin and delegated all its responsibilities back to the Bundesbank; the Fed has also been mandated with systemic regulation in the US. Before June 2010, the UK had maintained its SIR structure – yet the Bank of England was establishing some mirror functions for systemic regulation, which include macroprudential analysis. With the ongoing tectonic shifts and debates, the sector, both on national and global scales, faces significant uncertainty over the coming decade and the prospects are bleak.

5.5 Selected Proposed Changes to Regulatory Bodies and to Banking Regulations

5.5.1 New or Reformed Regulatory Oversight: 'Uber' Structures

In its April 2009 summit the G7 broadened the mandate of a previously established body, the Financial Stability Forum (FSF) established in 1999 and renamed the entity the Financial Stability Board (FSB). The membership of the board includes national financial authorities (central banks, supervisory authorities, finance ministries); international financial institutions (BIS, ECB, EC, IMF, WB, OECD), international standard setters and committees of central bank experts (BCBS; IAIS; IOSCO; IASB; CGFS; CPSS). The board's mandate is to

a) assess vulnerabilities affecting the financial system, b) identify and oversee action needed to address them, c) promote coordination and information sharing among authorities responsible for financial stability, d) monitor and advise on market developments, e) advise on and monitor best practice in meeting regulatory standards, f) collaborate with the IMF, including in conducting early warning exercises, g) undertake joint strategic reviews of the policy development work of the international standard setting bodies, h) set guidelines for and support supervisory colleges and i) come up with contingency planning for cross-border crisis management (particularly for systemically important firms). Two key themes are underscored by the board: first that 'there is no single silver bullet', that a combination of approaches to assess and address systemic risks is needed. Second: 'no one size fits all' – the choice of policy action has to be determined by the structure, the size of the financial system, nature and extent of domestic and cross-border linkages and the status of the institution as being subject to the 'home' or 'host' jurisdictions (i.e. it is an independent subsidiary, with the mother company not liable for its deposits or liabilities, or merely a branch, with all the regulatory implications thereof).

Other 'super' regulators also set up in 2009, include the European Systemic Risk Board at a European level, while in the US more powers were delegated to the Fed. The mandate of the ESRB is the macroprudential oversight of the financial system within the European Union. It aims to prevent and mitigate systemic risks in the financial system within the European system to prevent financial distress. It is also charged with issuing risk warnings, giving recommendations on measures and following-up on implementation. The Risk Board will have 33 full members: the 27 EU central bank governors, the ECB president and vice-president, a Commission member and the three chairs of the new European Supervisory Authorities – the European Banking Authority (EBA), the European Insurance and Occupational Pensions Authority (EIOPA) and the European Securities Authority (ESA). A representative from one national supervisory authority or each EU country may attend the meetings of the ESRB, but – to ensure close cooperation – will have no voting rights.

5.5.2 New Markets

A centralized clearing house for a segment of the CDS market was expected to be fully operational towards the end of 2009. The clearing house would ensure that for any given participant, all transactions on the same underlying entity would be netted to a single position, and a single margin account maintained on its entire portfolio of CDS. Bringing OTC derivatives on to regulated exchanges and standardizing the instruments, should help enhance transparency and market discipline. The caveat of course, is that some of these instruments are highly structured or tailored to the needs of specific investors, so standardization might not be feasible and/or desirable. In addition, these instruments offer a lucrative reward for banks offering them to a large extent because of their inherent opacity.

5.6 Selected Proposed Changes to Regulation

In 2009 the Basle Committee for Banking Supervision (BCBS) and the International Association of Deposit Insurers (IADI) proposed the following changes to restore the level and quality of bank capital in 2009:

1. Higher (and better quality) risk-weighted capital requirements
    Capital adequacy requirements should dictate banks holding more capital as compared to the risk profile of their assets not only in terms of the ratio of capital to be held but also the quality of this capital.
2. Countercyclical credit-loss provisioning
    Provisioning rules that would require banks to take more provisions in 'good' times, at the upturn of the credit cycle and 'less' provisions when times are bad, at the downturn of the credit cycle.
3. Formal leverage ratio
    Formal leverage ratio to 'cap' the extent of leverage banks can engage in, in addition to the minimum capital requirements. Such ratios are commonly used by multi-lateral development institutions and domestic development institutions.
4. Mandatory capital insurance or contingent capital
    Capital reserves that could be 'called upon' when they are needed, whether it be in the form of insurance, capital notes with a certain structure, or reserves of a special nature.
5. Convertible capital
    Hybrid debt or hybrid capital notes, convertible to capital.
6. Subordinated debt issuance frequency
    Put policies in place for the use of subordinated debt and its issuance frequency, again subject to leverage limits.
7. Prefunding of deposit insurance
    That deposit insurance be prefunded not on a 'pay as you go' basis, or the money to be provided in the case of a crisis (the money might not be available when a crisis hits).

8. Capital charges linked to systemic risk
    This is similar in concept to a systemic tax or that institutions with a large contribution to systemic risk pay an 'insurance' premium to the regulator. This tax or premium could fund a 'systemic risk fund' of sorts.

5.6.1 Countercyclical Regulation and Lean Against the Wind (LATW) Policies

The main causes of the previous crisis were an asset price bubble and a credit boom, thus future policy making is geared towards countercyclical measures to ensure no repeats.

5.6.2 Tax Havens

Regulators are clamping down hard on tax havens to please the public as they have been the ones to bear the cost of the previous crisis, while high net worth and institutional investors reaped all the benefits and less of the downside. As discussed in an earlier section, while this is one of the arguments used by government officials to please crowds, I believe this issue should be evaluated on the basis of materiality: the trade-off between how much taxes these same organizations pay in tax jurisdictions as compared to how much they 'evade' on the back of their tax haven operations. The decision rule should be based on the net result to tax receipts, not how it is divided.

5.6.3 Bank Bonus Structures and Pay Caps

Major changes to bank bonus structures and pay caps were proposed, including longer vesting periods and stronger clawback provisions. The extent of the regulation of pay structures should be carefully evaluated on a cost-to-benefit basis to ensure that this does not result in easily executed 'regulatory arbitrage' tactics by bankers.

5.6.3a Bank Living Wills

Regulators are calling for banks to draw their own resolution plans for key strategic businesses which kick into action when and if their resolution is needed. This would be very useful in a crisis resolution situation, provided that the exercise is undertaken in earnest by the banks not as a remote or improbable event.

5.6.3b Bank Systemic Tax

A systemic tax on large institutions with a high systemic impact is proposed by leading academics. The idea is that an institution which contributes more to overall systemic risk should pay a mandatory 'systemic insurance premium'. This is the same as the BCBS proposition.

5.6.3c Taxation of Financial Transactions in the US

A proposal was made to impose taxes on financial transactions by the various regulators to generate some USD150 billion.

5.6.3d IOSCO Proposed Regulation of Financial Products

IOSCO is considering expanding its regulatory scope to include more direct supervision of investment products, credit rating agencies and hedge funds.

Chapter 6

THE WAY FORWARD, MACROPRUDENTIAL ANALYSIS AND EARLY WARNING SYSTEMS FOR FRAGILITY AND CRISES

Turner (2009) and the IMF analyses indicate that the length of the recession post a banking stress episode is eight quarters on average, versus only three quarters for recessions which are not preceded by financial stress. So in addition to all the earlier motivation presented in preceding chapters thus far, this further highlights the impact of large imbalance build-up on cost and duration of a crisis and hence the need to indentify a crisis at a 'pre-crisis' time, namely the build-up of imbalances at the stage of financial fragility. This is the role early warning systems (EWS) should play. This chapter starts with a general conceptual discussion of early warning systems for crises and the required elements for a robust system, followed by a historical survey of EWS design and concludes with an evaluation of how well existing models predicted the past crisis.

6.1 General Conceptual Design and Elements of a Robust and Applicable EWS

A robust and applicable EWS is a cornerstone of any sound framework for ensuring financial sector stability. S. Lall et al. (2008) identify the following elements: pre-crisis sanctions on undercapitalized financial institutions that pose systemic risks (in this respect the importance of a thorough stress- and back-testing framework directly linked to macroprudential regulation is needed. During the past crisis, the usefulness of this tool was short sold all too prematurely); legal and institutional mechanisms to deal quickly with weak financial institutions; and an effective deposit insurance system.

The IMF cautions though that EWS systems are not a substitute for *sound and balanced judgements* on financial weaknesses.

The EWS also needs to be *usable* by policy makers in a practical manner. Borio & Drehmann (2009) underscore the importance of applicability and the need to take the policy maker's objectives into account when designing an EWS. Thus the choice of models and the selection of thresholds taking into account the trade-off between correctly calling crises and false alarms (what is commonly referred to in the literature as noise-to-signal ratios) should be tailored to the policy makers' objectives. They also identify that one of the design features of an effective EWS should be the clear quantitative delineation of the definition of a crisis (e.g. indirect cost of failures as a percentage of GDP, a bank run on a specific percentage of bank deposits is what the system would classify as a crisis, or others, but a clear 'crisis' objective which can be measured). The advantage of a quantifiable objective as such is that it would also enable cross-border objective comparisons as well as standardized time series analysis. Karim & Davis (2008) stipulate two further conditions for an *effective* EWS: having sufficient lead time to allow the policy maker to take action and that it is *simple* enough to be understood by policy makers at all levels.

The usefulness of such an EWS, the authors continue, is that it would enable authorities to warn financial market players of potential risks in speeches and various publications and also alert bank examiners that they need to do more thorough examinations at times of elevated stress. A *credible* EWS would also justify direct policy action to avoid a crisis by policy makers through the use of prudential measures on lending to certain sectors or in the form of monetary and macro action.

6.2 History of EWS Design

EWS are used to i) identify the macro states where policy action is needed (macro-models), ii) provide a rating system of individual institutions for a peer group or financial system in a country or indeed globally (micro-models), and iii) map the choice of policy tools to reduce crises costs.

6.2.1 Identify the States Where Policy Action is Needed (Macro-Models)

The evolution of EWS historically follows through from the evolution of their theoretical underpinnings which dictate the design to trace the hypothesized causes of crises. The theory on banking crises is usually categorized according to four generations (Breuer 2004).

First-generation models (for example Mishkin, 1978), hypothesize that a poor macroeconomic setting adversely affects banks' borrowers and in turn impacts the depositors themselves, resulting in bank runs which ultimately lead to the closure of financial institutions.

Second-generation models focus on depositor behaviour and regard banking crises as 'sunspot' events or self-fulfilling prophecies, unrelated to the business cycle.

Third-generation models highlight the role played by boom and bust cycles in the economy (and twin crises – a twin crisis is when there is a simultaneous balance of payments or currency crisis coupled with a banking crisis, e.g. the Asian crisis in 1998), with banking problems arising on the asset side of the institutions being fuelled by excessive lending against collateral such as real estate and equities. A bust cycle then causes asset prices to fall, financial institutions to lend less and a credit crunch to develop, which leads to further economic slowdown and more borrower defaults.

Finally, *fourth-generation* models seek to identify the features of the institutional environment that set the stage for the build-up of macroeconomic imbalances, which then gives rise to banking problems.

A multitude of empirical models to assess such indicators have been developed in two main strands: models which rely on macroeconomic indicators as key explanatory variables and models that asses how microeconomic factors contribute to banking crises. These were followed by a number of integrated empirical models which took both types of explanatory variables into account. These models use different methodologies and either predict individual bank failure or look at systemic banking crises as a whole. The methodologies mainly fall into *four* categories: a) signals models (which include sub-branches of first-generation, second-generation and third-generation type models), b) logit/probit models, iii) Merton-type models and a less-used class of models, d) binary recursive trees.

6.2.1a Selected Macro-Models

In Austria the Oesterreichische Nationalbank (OeNB) uses a proprietary model for systemic risk analysis and stress testing of the banking system. Boss, Krenn, Puhr and Summer (2006) outline the key features of this model with the building blocks comprising market risk, non-interbank credit risk and an interbank network model. The factors chosen for each building block are the ones which maximize out-of-sample performance. The output of this model consists of problem statistics of the banking system, identification of fundamental versus contagion-type potential problem events and a value at risk for the lender of last resort or 'price tag' for intervention.

In the UK, the Bank of England also uses a network type model, but focusing on a set of *six identified vulnerabilities*, while recognizing that other vulnerabilities might not be identified or measured. The model then attempts to analyze the ways that a potential shock could trigger each vulnerability and identify which sub-sectors of the financial and non-financial sector will be affected It also seeks to find out what the second-order effects and feedback effects between the real economy and the financial sector are and the impact of the combined effects of transmission channels.

6.2.2 Provide a Rating System of Individual Institutions (Micro-Models)

Micro-models, which identify states where policy action is required and whose output is mainly the identification of systemic hot spots, were supplemented by central banks and agencies to provide rating systems of institutions within their jurisdiction on a micro-level. These include, but are not limited to, analyses of capital adequacy, asset quality, management, efficiency, liquidity and sensitivities to various risks, commonly called CAMELS for short, analysis rankings of financial institutions, and all derivatives thereof. I believe that the former macro-models could also be applied to identify individual institution vulnerabilities and in turn rankings. By doing so, this will provide a more consistent and macro-approach for systemic and individual institution analysis.

Poghosyan and Cihak (2009) provide a comprehensive survey of EWS used by European regulators, utilizing a unique database of individual bank distress across the European Union from the mid-1990s to 2008 on the basis of which they identify a set of indicators (CAMELS based) and thresholds to distinguish between sound banks and banks vulnerable to financial distress. They highlight the usefulness of an *EU-level early warning system* based on this model, with published results by banks compared by benchmarks to enhance market discipline. The dataset is based on Bankscope data, on 5,708 banks, plus information obtained from NewsPlus/Factiva on each bank with regards to any financial support or other forms of rescue or merger. The authors identify 79 distress events for 54 banks. Using a Logit model they find that the model would have correctly called more than 55% to 68% of distress cases. The explanatory variables they find most useful are: *capitalization, asset quality* and *profitability*. While cost-to-income ratios and basic liquidity indicators failed poorly (a liquidity indicator which measures wholesale percentage financing of liabilities was useful, however). They also find depositor discipline has an important signalling effect (if a bank pays higher rates on its deposits than its competitors, it has a higher probability of distress).

6.3 Performance of these Models: Did they Predict the Crisis?

Did the quantitative EWS models described in the preceding sections predict the current crisis and ensuing global meltdown with losses exceeding trillions of dollars or is there an element related to non-quantifiable issues as 'gambling and looting' and other behavioural issues that could not have been mapped? Asli Demirgüç-Kunt and Enrica Detragiache (2005), Kane (1989) and Akerlof and Romer (1993) had dubbed the US savings and loans crisis in the 1980s as such an episode. They demonstrated how the erosion of bank capital following financial liberalization, generous deposit insurance and ineffective regulation conspired to make 'gambling and looting' an optimal strategy for scores of bank managers. Other cases of systemic wide crises which resulted from fraud are Venezuela (1994), and Guinea in 1985 where the six main banks, accounting for over 95% of the system, were closed on a single day on the back of widespread bank fraud (Honohan 1997).

Davis & Karim (2008) try to assess whether EWS based on a) logit and b) binomial tree, binary recursive trees (BRT) approaches for the UK and US economies could have helped raise the alarm about an impending crisis before the recent crisis. They also consider a 'checklist approach' of indicators previously used. They find that the models were *not* largely successful and as such suggest *a broadening of the approach to a more comprehensive set of macroprudential analyses.* They start with a survey of the various financial stability reviews (IMF, ECB, Bank of England and BIS) in the spring of 2007 to gauge whether any of them showed concern over an impending crisis. They find that *collectively* these reports did point out: deterioration in credit quality of US subprime mortgages; high European institutions' exposure to the US subprime market; rising corporate leverage; rising household indebtedness; rising capital flows into emerging markets; concerns about credit-risk transfer between markets; high asset prices and irrational exuberance; complacency by LCFIs; poor perception of risk due to the 'originate and distribute' model; the potential of liquidity 'vanishing' from markets; a likely rise in investor's risk aversion in the case of a shock and most importantly a significant deviation from historic norms for many of these indicators. The BIS concluded that 'a tail event affecting the global economy might at some point have much higher costs than is commonly supposed'. Thus while the features of the crisis were correctly recognized on a collective level, the extent was not. It is worth noting, however, that the Bank of England's FSR of April 2007correctly identified most of the key vulnerabilities to include the major causes of the recent crises and estimated a potential loss of UK bank's tier I capital of up to 30% to 40% (or GBP47 billion to GBP62 billion), given certain scenarios, an estimate which was spot on for the first-order-effects of the crisis.

If these bodies had conducted a combined stress test with all the fragilities identified, would have they been able to predict the crisis and correctly estimate its magnitude? Would this have acted as a deterrent to the US before it allowed the collapse of Lehman Brothers in September of 2008? This view is supported by Borio and Drehmann (2008) who identify crucial features of an operational framework to address financial instability as including setting up institutional arrangements that leverage the comparative expertise of the various authorities involved in safeguarding financial stability. It is worth mentioning that none of these bodies included an analysis of SIVs, a key feature in this crisis.

Using a sample of 105 countries and covering the years 1979 to 2003, Davis & Karim (2008) apply the models to US and UK data to test for out-of-sample performance from 2000–2007 (they partition the sample first into a sub-set until 1999, and the rest). In both cases, they set the start date of the crisis as 2007. They find that for the US, both models fail miserably with a probability of a crisis occurring in 2007 of 1% predicted by the logit model and 0.6% predicted by the binary tree model. For the UK, the results were similar, with logit model predicting the probability of a crisis at 3.4% in 2007 and the binary tree model assigning a 0.6% probability of a crisis occurring.. The authors identify a short checklist approach for detecting financial instability, including a) regime shifts, b) entry conditions, c) debt accumulation, 4) innovation in financial markets, and 5) risk concentration.

Alessi and Detken (2009) find *that out-of-sample performance of a set of global liquidity indicators* would have predicted the most recent wave of *asset price booms* (2005–2007). These include global private credit, long-term nominal bond yield, housing investment, short-term nominal interest rate, real equity price index and real GDP.

A 2006 IMF review of EWS in use and the next steps forward concludes that EWS models have *shown mixed results in terms of forecasting accuracy*, but nevertheless offer a systematic, objective and consistent method to predict crises which avoids analysts' biases. It also stresses the importance of developing a set of building blocks to predict foreign exchange crises, debt crises, sovereign risk, banking crises, financial market linkages/spillovers, and contagion and crosscountry linkages. Bell and Pain (2000), after reviewing the existing EWS models up till 2000, with a special application to the Asian crisis, conclude that the models are subject to some significant weaknesses and limitations, especially as potential tools for policy makers.

Gunther and Moore (2002) analyze EWS in real time using a probit approach and identify as such *one reason why EWS have performed so poorly*. This study is interesting in that it uses a unique set of banking data over 1996 through to 1998 which includes both originally reported and revised financial variables for 12 financial ratios based on CAMELS. They find adverse revisions to initially reported data to be associated with downgrades in supervisory ratings. As such these results highlight the auditing role of bank exams and the implications thereof on a realistic assessment of EWS model accuracy. If the data on which an EWS is based is revised, then naturally the original output of the model was distorted. In a related study, O'Keefe et al (2003) stress the importance of loan underwriting practices in the determination of bank credit risk and study the relationship between examiners' assessments of the riskiness of bankers' lending practices and subsequent changes in the riskiness of bank portfolios. The authors investigate whether examiner assessments should as such serve as aids to an EWS which is based on real time data. They find that higher (lower) risk in underwriting practices is indeed associated with subsequent increases (decreases) in non-performing assets generally.

Chapter 7

REGULATORY TUMBLEWEED
OR IS IT TANGLEWEED?

7.1 EWS Implications for Regulation

Global leaders in the aftermath of the current crisis have underscored the importance of an EWS.

'An early warning system must be established to identify upstream increases in risks...'
—*Heads of State or Government of European Union, November 7, 2008*

'The Group recommends that the IMF, in close cooperation with other interested bodies ... is put in charge of developing and operating a financial stability early warning system, accompanied by an international risk map and credit register. The early warning system should aim to deliver clear messages to policy makers and to recommend pre-emptive policy responses ...'
—*De Larosière Report, 25 February, 2009*

7.1.2 *The Role of EWS in Directing Policy Action Design and Tools*

Given the prohibitive cost of crises, a number of studies were conducted to empirically assess crosscountry intervention policies to determine which policies could minimize the costs of crises and should therefore be utilized, and which measures increase the costs and should be avoided. Honohan and Klingebiel (2003) constructed a database with 40 banking crises and the respective policy responses by governments according to five categories: a) blanket guarantees to depositors, b) liquidity support to banks, c) bank recapitalization, d) financial assistance to debtors and 5) forbearance. The authors link the various intervention policies and the fiscal cost of the bailout and *find that the more generous bailouts had higher fiscal costs as expected*. Claessens, Klingebiel and Laeven (2004) find that these generous bailouts do *not reduce* the output cost of banking crises as measured by the output loss relative to trend during the crisis period. Both studies endorse the view that the high moral hazard associated with bailouts which are too generous is more detrimental than effective – the question is how can regulators determine what is too generous in the middle of a crisis?

Hoggarth and Reidhill (2003) survey various measures of reducing the net costs of crisis resolution and of reducing the probability of future crises. They outline a number of qualitative measures including the preferable use of private sector solutions, loss imposition on bank stakeholders and shareholders to reduce moral hazard, increasing transparency and disclosure of resolution programmes in general, minimizing forbearance and expediting resolution. They also explore the various resolution strategies and their cost impact including: unassisted resolutions (bank status remains the same or is changed/ private sector merger), liquidation and assisted resolutions (bank status remains the same, open bank assistance, bank status changed, bridge banks, outright government ownership). Santomero and Hoffman (1998) provide a similar survey that focuses on three distinct case studies in this respect, US banks, Scandinavian banks and French banks, arriving at the same conclusions as Hogarth and Reidhill.

7.1.2a Necessary vs Sufficient Policy Measures

Kaufman (2001) notes that in times of credit crunch, the whole economy contracts. If the government tries to force it out of a contraction through too much intervention using policy tools, coercing banks to increase lending could have negative consequences because it only weakens the banks further by making them extend excessively risky loans and exacerbates the size of the problem in the long run. He depicts the lifecycle of market-government regulation as follows:

Market regulation ⟶ market failures ⟶ 'horror stories' ⟶ government intervention (regulation) ⟶ government failures ⟶ government deregulation ⟶ market regulation ⟶ market failure.

While government policy actions are necessary, as seen from Kaufman's depiction, they are not sufficient. Sufficiency would stem from the revamping of financial stability frameworks and other structural reforms which will ensure a sounder and safer system in the long run. Also more streamlining of global financial stability frameworks and strengthening frameworks in developing and emerging countries is needed as where or when the next crisis will hit remains unknown. Even though there are a number of robust frameworks in developed countries; the need for streamlining and further cooperation cross-border has been highlighted by the recent crisis. Also financial stability

Figure 7.1. Policy Tools Used in Crisis Resolution for 33 Systemic Banking Crises and Resulting Cumulative Fiscal Costs – An Evaluation (1977–2002).

	No. Of Crises	Avg Length of Crisis (years)	Non-performing Loans (% of total loans)	Bank Credit/Annual GDP (Avg %)	Avg GNP per capita (000's, PPP based, at crisis start)	Cumulative fiscal costs of banking resolution (% of GDP), Avg.	Output Losses 1 (% of GDP), median	Output Losses 2 (% of GDP), median
All countries	**33**	**4.3**	**26.7**	**44.2**	**6.6**	**15**	**7.1**	**23.1**
LOLR (open-ended)								
- Yes	21	4.8	31.1	47.1	6.7	17.3	13.9	37
- No	12	3.4	19.3	39.1	6.4	10.9	3.8	9.1
Blanket deposit guarantee								
- Yes	22	4.3	29.3	47.8	7.9	16.6	9.8	28.7
- No	11	4.3	17.3	37	4	11.8	5	15.7
Banking Crisis alone	**10**	**4.6**	**23.7**	**44.9**	**7.3**	**7.8**	**2.4**	**15.7**
Banking & Currency Crisis	**23**	**4.2**	**28.2**	**43.9**	**6.3**	**17.4**	**11.6**	**32.2**
of which:								
- with LOLR	16	4.5	32.9	45.1	5.9	18.9	17	43.9
- without LOLR	7	3.4	17.5	41.3	7.3	14.1	4.8	13.2
of which:								
- with blanket deposit guarantee	16	3.9	29.7	46.9	7.5	19.4	17	37.2
- without blanket deposit guarantee	7	4.9	19.5	37.1	3.6	12.8	4.8	24.7

Source: Hoggarth and Reidhill, 2003.

frameworks will need to be brought up to international best practice in developing and emerging markets, with the developed world in poor economic health and suffering from an ageing population, banks will have to start expanding more in these countries looking for growth. Another motivation would be regulatory arbitrage for operations set up in countries with weak regulators compared to strong home country regulation. As the operations of banks grow in developing and emerging markets, ensuring developed countries' stability will in part have to be addressed by ensuring stability of developing markets. This is clearly demonstrated by the Dubai World credit-risk transfer example, with a 'problem' exposure by Standard Chartered and HSBC of USD26 billion. More recently, problems have emerged with a large Saudi business conglomerate, Al Saad Group, which reportedly has USD20 billion in problem loans owed to local and international players, for which it offered 8 cents to the dollar to its creditors during attempted settlement negotiations which broke down. This development is foreseen by Kaufman's (2001) empirical evaluation over three decades, whereby, he notes that since 1973, losses from banking crises as a percent of GDP were nearly four times as great in emerging economies which had poor financial stability frameworks – providing open-ended financial support to their banks – than countries that provided smaller or no such support.

7.1.3 Procyclicality and Boundary Problems in Financial Regulation: A Meta-Theory for Guiding New EWS Design?

What is the meta-space comprised of for a design of an effective EWS? What are the tradeoffs? Four main elements of this meta-space are: a) regulator objectives: price stability versus financial stability, b) macroprudential versus microprudential analysis, c) procyclical versus countercyclical measures, and d) rules-based versus risk-based regulation.

i) **Regulator Objectives: Price Stability vs Financial Stability**

Goodhart et al (2006) present the various tradeoffs between central banks' objectives of price stability versus financial stability and the implications thereof. In terms of price stability, measurement and definition is established, the instruments for control are present, there is a high degree of accountability, there is a forecasting structure based on central tendencies and a simple administrative procedure is in place. In terms of financial stability there are many challenges in measurement and definition, control tools, accountability, forecasting and administrative procedures. Consequently, designing EWS which address the latter is a challenging task given the 'fluid' nature of the components. *This would necessarily also imply that the 'optimal' EWS also be of a dynamic and 'fluid' nature within each sub-category in order to satisfy regulator objectives.*

ii) Macroprudential versus microprudential analysis

Borio (2006) delineates the tradeoffs in both analysis approaches. A macroprudential approach takes into account correlations and common exposures among institutions, whereas a microprudential approach focuses only on individual institutions. *For an EWS design to be effective, it has to take into account both types of analysis to ensure completeness and a comprehensive mapping of risk on a 'gross' and 'net' basis, after taking into account the eliminated or offset risks within a system, and the positive or negative impact of having a strong or weak regulator, respectively.*

iii) Procyclical versus countercyclical measures

Goodhart (2008) explores procyclical versus countercyclical measures through a discussion of the boundary problem in financial regulation. He reiterates his proposal that *state and time-varying capital adequacy requirements are needed* (similar to the Spanish model) through a discussion of how and where to set the boundary for regulation. Too much regulation could result in disintermediation, competitive inequality (no level-playing-field), and inefficiency and higher spreads. Wadhwani (2008) finds that there are strong theoretical and empirical reasons for considering a 'lean-against-the-wind' (LATW), countercyclical tilt to monetary policy to enhance macroeconomic stability. He discusses Bernanke's proposition on the difficulty of 'safe popping' an asset bubble without grave consequences on the economy. He also cites one case, Sweden, where LATW actually worked. With house prices increasing drastically in Sweden, on a few occasions in 2004–5, the Riksbank did for that reason lean against the wind and did not take rates down as quickly as they could have considering the outlook for inflation alone. *Thus for an EWS to be 'implementable', it has to give sufficient lead time to enable countercyclical/LATW policy action and also identify the most effective tools for policy action as such.*

iv) Rules-based versus risk-based regulation

The roll-out of Basle II in 2004 and its global adoption by banks starting 2007, with full compliance originally expected by 2010, has been blamed for increasing procyclicality and hence exacerbating the recent crisis. However, if Basle II had been adopted in its entirety, before the crisis had developed, it would have achieved its initial objectives of a introducing a more *risk-sensitive* capital measurement and minimum regulatory capital requirement and a *'risk-based' regulations* and supervision framework as opposed to a 'rules-based' framework of regulation and supervision. Basle II's three pillars are a self-contained framework with its own internal checks and balances. The main problem was that only Pillar I was being

Figure 7.2. Tradeoffs between Regulator Objectives and Macroprudential vs Microprudential Analysis.

	Price Stability	Financial Stability
Measurement & Definition	Yes, subject to technical queries	Hardly, except by its absence
Instrument for Control	Yes, subject to lags	Limited, and difficult to adjust
Accountable	Yes	Hardly
Forecasting Structure	Central tendency of distribution	Tails of distribution
Forecasting Procedure	Standard Froecasts	Simulations or Stress
Administrative Procedure	Simple	Difficult

	Macroprudential	Microprudential
Proximate Objective	limit financial system-wide distress	Hardly, except by its absence
Ultimate Objective	avoid output (GDP) costs	Limited, and difficult to adjust
Characterisation of risk	(in part) endogenous	Hardly
Correlations & common exposures across institutions	important	exogenous
calibration of prudential controls	in terms of system-wide risk; top-down	in terms of risks of individual institutions; bottom-up

Source: Goodhart et al (2006), Borio (2006).

rolled out, while Pillars II and III were still 'playing catch-up'. Pillar II, on supervision, through the use of stress testing, gives regulators the tool to enforce minimum capital requirements on the basis of *differentiated risk exposures* of various institutions, discarding Basle I's 'one-size-fits-all' approach. Pillar III on market discipline would ensure that whatever is not addressed by Pillars, I and II is captured by the 'market'. For the most recent crisis, it's my view that we had a failure of pillars II and III, rather than pillar I. Pillar II's stress tests, albeit not sufficient without adding an additional component for liquidity stress tests and for back testing as well, never got the chance to be utilized, and regulators were still trying to fully comprehend the various models used by banks under the internal ratings based (IRB) approach. While pillar III on market discipline was undermined in two key ways. Firstly in scope, it was not generic enough to require that systemically significant markets in which banks are active must be subject to a minimum level of accepted transparency and disclosure on their operations. With notional outstanding value of the global derivatives markets at more than ten times global GDP and more than twenty times global banking assets, these markets should have been subject to minimum transparency and disclosure. Secondly, by not acknowledging the weaknesses inherent in markets given that the built-in assumptions of rationality and efficiency necessary for market functioning do not hold all the time. If we do not assume that markets are rational or efficient, then a world with market dislocations is possible and we always have to be on our toes so to speak – there is no room for complacency and for trusting the markets to continuously self-correct without financial collapses. The 'Great Moderation' of Robert Lucas, and the premise of Alan Greenspan's monetary policy easing is a myth, markets do not self-correct and they can suffer from severe dislocations. Working on this basis, Pillar III would have signalled to regulators that shifts they saw in the market pre-crisis needed to be investigated more thoroughly or that 'something might be wrong' and the market is trying to tell us something. In my view, as far as Basle II is concerned, the ranking of the causes of the past crisis would be market discipline followed by a significant lag of failures in pillars II and I, respectively. *The global banking sector was simply too big to FRAME: fail, regulate, audit, manage and evaluate.*

It follows then that in a risk-based regulatory setup, the role of the regulator is far more paramount to the safe-guarding of a system's stability, much more so than in a simple rules-based setup. *A weak regulator would in effect jeopardize a strong system and a strong regulator would strengthen a weak system.* This is illustrated visually by Figure 7.3.

Figure 7.3. Financial System 'Net Risk': Regulator Strength and System Fragility.

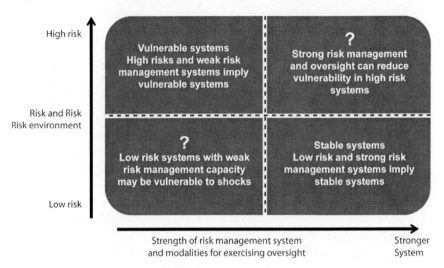

Sources: Johnston, Chai and Schumacher (2000).

7.2 Critique of Proposed Changes

Focusing on frameworks and power struggles as opposed to what actually gets accomplished on the ground is one of the main hurdles to the effectiveness of regulation. Furthermore, based on empirical research, having separate regulators (SIRs) as opposed to (TPs) for financial agents is precisely what results in information asymmetries. Creating new bodies creates new asymmetries.

The banking sector prior to the crisis was highly concentrated, and after the crisis it will be even more so, which brings to the forefront the concept of not only too big to fail (TBTF) to another level, but what I would like to redub, as I clearly illustrated by various metrics throughout this book, too big to **FRAME** – fail, regulate, audit, manage and evaluate. Furthermore, business cycles are mostly national – what implications does this have on the implementation of countercyclical measures for LCFIs?

Similarly, criticism of addressing so-called 'crowd pleasers' such as tax havens and bonus structures have been made and rightly so: there must always be a trade-off between materiality and regulation. Prior to the crisis, irrespective of the level of bonuses, most bank employees actually kept their holdings in the form of shares in their banks, how could caps on payouts as such improve incentives? The UK's bankers bonus tax collected GBP2 billion on year 2009 bonuses, distributed in 2010 (compared to around GBP100 billion directly invested in banks in the UK to shore up their capital). How much time did this exercise take from regulators and would it not have been better to focus that time on more turning around the part-nationalized banks?

Thus, while the global financial regulatory reform agenda is ambitious in its objectives, an important design element should ensure *effectiveness* of regulation and remove information asymmetries between same country and cross-border regulators. How do they face the tumbleweed blowing their way?

7.3 Blowing Tumbleweed or is it Tangleweed? Focal Points to Address

The scope of changes in regulatory issues is unfathomable and some of the finest minds working with regulators, specific regulators in charge of sizable markets, academics, international policy development institutions, industry associations and government bodies, among many others are engaged in their redesign. I think regardless of which body deals with what and ends up having more regulatory 'power', some basic focal points need to be covered and the final 'form', framework', 'tools' and indeed 'executers' will then naturally fall into place for a safer and sounder system if these points are indeed addressed.

7.3.1 Greater Market Discipline

The last crisis showed clearly that regulators need to better understand what is happening in their financial markets. One way to achieve this would be through *greater market discipline*, sharing more with participants and players on a national level and *publicly* warning against eminent threats. Sharing information publicly with the market through preset regular schedules via publications, presentations and hearings at national assemblies should ensure *effectiveness*. If regulators have to report their performance, then it will improve automatically. Greater market discipline should be used as a tool bearing in mind that for it to be effective, its scope should include all systemically significant markets and these need to have a minimum level of accepted transparency and disclosure. Also that markets are neither necessarily always efficient nor rational, deviations should be investigated diligently.

7.3.2 Staying Close to Industry Players

Regulators need to leave their 'ivory towers' and communicate closely with industry players to understand the businesses their players are involved in, how they are making their profits and the risks they are accumulating in the process. More importantly, they must be on very good terms with the leaders of systemically significant institutions on a personal level. Integrity again cannot be underscored, size and balance sheet strength mean nothing if you cannot trust the business ethic of the clan leader.

7.3.3 Discouraging 'Group Think' and Protection of Whistle-Blowers

Another important design aspect is the governance structures of regulators, discouraging group think and protecting whistle-blowers, the more balanced to ensure a diversity of opinions, the better. Strengthening the whistle-blower channel means that differing views can and will be heard. Also ensuring adequate representation from the private sector on regulatory boards and sufficient 'brainstorming' open up discussions with the private sector on upcoming regulations and existing regulations. Listening to views from think tanks and independent economists is also crucial in ensuring regulators are not divorced from the market.

7.3.4 Burden Sharing, Moral Hazard

Businesses succeed or fail and the same applies to financial institutions. Each stakeholder in a business should always share the 'burden' commensurate to the nature of its stake holding. Thus equity shareholders, with unlimited upside, should also pay for the costs of getting wiped out. Likewise with debt holders, an investor – though only getting a fixed return on its debt – should expect repayment, prior to equity shareholders receiving any funds in the case of failure. Any exceptions will result in playing fields which are not level.

7.3.5 Going Back to the Basics: Prudence and Modesty

Investors, especially those in charge of money belonging to others, have a fiduciary duty not only to make the best investments for their clients on an absolute-return basis, but also on a risk-adjusted basis. Agents and principal investors should apply prudence and undertake necessary due diligence before embarking on an investment. An investor should understand what they are investing in, the mapping of the returns and the risks and if they don't then perhaps a degree of modesty is required and opportunities forgone if necessary.

7.3.6 Ethics, Ethics, Ethics

Inclusion of a strong ethical code of conduct and ethics training for both regulators and private sector players is crucial – if anything the last crisis was also a clear crisis of ethics and governance. If mortgage brokers had not extended loans to people who could not repay them, then the subprime market would have not collapsed and the crisis would possibly not have occurred. If mortgage brokers had extended these loans, but we had much lower leverage levels because banks were not seeking extra yield at any cost, then the crisis would have been nowhere close to what it was in terms of magnitude. If investment officers were not overzealous in investing in products for which they did not perform sufficient due diligence because they were following the herd, the magnitude of the spillover would have been much less.

In short, if people had better ethics, we would never have crises, period, because excesses would not develop and because if they do, they would be reported and acted upon before it is too late. Ethics have a quantifiable value, and their value is derived from a complete default scenario. Without ethics, all contractual obligations would not be worth the paper they are written on and indeed markets cannot function. I have demonstrated this throughout this book and I believe that the argument would be valid to all crises which have occurred in the past, whether they be financial or otherwise.

7.3.7 EWS and Analytic Tools: Maintaining the Logic

Each crisis will be different, have different triggers and unravel in a different manner to its predecessors. The problem is, as human beings, our perception is always skewed towards what we have seen in our own lifetimes; we do not learn from history and markets do have a short-term memory (we are not capable of seeing 'black swans'). Therefore the best way to prevent a crisis is to ensure that the 'system' is as healthy as possible by attacking imbalances before they accumulate, and recognizing that you cannot predict crises or their timing using a rear-view mirror calibrated model.

A model will only help capture imbalance build-up. Yes it is *necessary* as a *starting point*, however it is nowhere near sufficient, it has to be approached as part of *a set of decision suites to be used*, the rest is up to human judgement, common sense, grounded modesty and ethical action. I am not underestimating the importance of analytics, on the contrary, I am stressing their necessity as a *starting point* and that decisions be made based on proper and insightful analysis. I am, as such, calling for *perspective* in their use and a focus on achieving 'regulatory effectiveness' through their application.

Given this perspective, the importance of a strong macroprudential surveillance and systemic regulator function with wide reaching powers to safeguard against financial instability is paramount. Having a robust early warning signals system (EWS) in place is the core 'brain' component of such a system. It will serve in satisfying two key goals in the oversight of systemic financial stability: a) limiting financial system-wide distress, and b) avoiding output or GDP costs. The earlier and more reliable this system is in predicting instability – and the more easily understood, mapped and shared with a high degree of transparency among the parties concerned with safeguarding financial stability in any country and indeed across borders – the more likely it will achieve its objectives by allowing sufficient lead time for action. The past crisis highlighted the global nature of shocks and thus a global EWS is needed to assess and disseminate key threats to financial stability and information on systemic vulnerabilities in a quantifiable manner. By so doing the EWS will assist policy makers in preventing crises, in a financial world with more integrity and more ethics.

Appendix 1

CURRENT CRISIS TIME LOG ACROSS THE GLOBE

Appendix 1: Crisis Time Log Across the Globe
Pages 128–42

Date	US	UK	Europe	Others
3-Jan-07	Ownit Mortgage Solutions Inc. files for Chapter 11. Records show that Ownit Mortgage Solutions owed Merrill Lynch around USD93 million at the time of filing.			
5-Feb-07	Mortgage Lenders Network USA Inc., the country's 15th largest subprime lender with USD3.3 billion in loans funded in third quarter 2006, files for Chapter 11.			
Feb-Mar 07	Subprime industry collapse; several subprime lenders declare bankruptcy; announcing significant losses or putting themselves up for sale. These include Accredited Home Lenders Holding, New Century Financial, DR Horton and Countrywide Financial.			

Appendix 1: Continued

Date	US	UK	Europe	Others
2-Apr-07	New Century Financial, the largest U.S. subprime lender, files for Chapter 11 bankruptcy.			
3-Apr-07	According to CNN Money, business sources report lenders made USD640 billion in subprime loans in 2006, nearly twice the level three years earlier; subprime loans amounted to about 20 percent of the nation's mortgage lending and about 17 percent of home purchases; financial firms and hedge funds likely own more than USD1 trillion in securities backed by subprime mortgage; about 13 percent of subprime loans are now delinquent, more than five times the delinquency rate for home loans to borrowers with top credit; more than 2 percent of subprime loans had foreclosure proceedings start in the fourth quarter of 2006.			

(Continued)

Appendix 1: Continued

Date	US	UK	Europe	Others
7-Jun-07	Bear Stearns & Co informs investors in two of its funds, the High-Grade Structured Credit Strategies Enhanced Leverage Fund and the High-Grade Structured Credit Fund, that it is halting redemptions			
20-Jun-07	Merrill Lynch seizes USD800 million in assets from two Bear Stearns hedge funds that were involved in securities backed by subprime loans.			
Aug-07	Sub-prime mortgage-backed securities are discovered in portfolios of banks and hedge funds around the world, from BNP Paribas to Bank of China. Many lenders stop offering home equity loans and "stated income" loans. Federal Reserve injects about USD100 billion into the money supply for banks to borrow at a low rate.			

Appendix 1: Continued

Date	US	UK	Europe	Others
6-Aug-07	American Home Mortgage Investment Corporation (AHMI) files for Chapter 11 bankruptcy. The company expects to see up to a USD60 million loss for the first quarter of 2007.			
8-Aug-07	Mortgage Guaranty Insurance Corporation (MGIC, Milwaukee, Wisconsin) announces it will discontinue its purchase of Radian Group after suffering a billion-dollar loss of its investment in Credit-Based Asset Servicing and Securitization (C-BASS, New York).			
9-Aug-07	French investment bank BNP Paribas suspends three investment funds that invested in subprime mortgage debt, due to a "complete evaporation of liquidity" in the market. The bank's announcement is the first of many credit-loss and write-down announcements by banks, mortgage lenders and other institutional investors.		European Central Bank pumps 95 billion euros into the European banking market.	

(Continued)

Appendix 1: Continued

Date	US	UK	Europe	Others
10-Aug-07	Central banks coordinate efforts to increase liquidity; the Federal Reserve (Fed) injects a combined USD43 billion.		ECB injects 156 billion euros of liquidity into European banking markets.	Bank of Japan injects 1 trillion Yen. Small amounts are injected by the central banks of Australia and Canada.
13-Aug-07	Sentinel Management Group suspends redemptions for investors and sells off USD312 million worth of assets; three days later Sentinel files for Chapter 11 bankruptcy.			
16-Aug-07	Countrywide Financial Corporation, the biggest US mortgage lender, narrowly avoids bankruptcy by taking out an emergency loan of USD11 billion from a group of banks.			
17-Aug-07	The Federal Reserve cuts the discount rate by half a percent to 5.75% from 6.25% while leaving the federal funds rate unchanged in an attempt to stabilize financial markets.			

Appendix 1: Continued

Date	US	UK	Europe	Others
31-Aug-07	President Bush announces a limited bailout of US homeowners unable to pay the rising costs of their debts. Ameriquest, one of the largest subprime lenders in the US, goes out of business.			
4-Sep-07	The Libor rate rises to its highest level since December 1998, at 6.7975%, above the Bank of England's 5.75% base rate.			
18-Sep-07	The Fed lowers interest rates by half a point (0.5%) to 5.25% in an attempt to limit damage to the economy from the housing and credit crises.			
30-Sep-07	Internet banking pioneer NetBank goes bankrupt.			
5-Oct-07	Merrill Lynch announces a USD5.5 billion loss as a consequence of the subprime crisis, which is revised to USD8.4 billion on 24 October.		Swiss bank UBS announces that it lost USD690 million in the third quarter.	

(Continued)

Appendix 1: Continued

Date	US	UK	Europe	Others
17-Oct-07	A consortium of US banks backed by the US government announces a "super fund" of USD100 billion to purchase mortgage-backed securities whose mark-to-market value plummeted in the subprime collapse.			
31-Oct-07	Fed lowers Fed Fund Rate by 25 bps to 4.5%.			
1-Nov-07	Fed injects USD41 billion into the money supply for banks to borrow at a low rate.			
24-Dec-07	Super-fund proposal abandoned, banks cite lack of demand for risky mortgage products.			
Jan 2008		Northern Rock, the UK's fifth largest mortgage lender, is nationalized, after a bank run where depositors withdrew EGB 1 billion or 4% of the bank's deposit base in one day.		
24-Jan-08			Societe Generale unveils GBP3.7 billion losses by rogue trader Jerome Kerviel.	

Appendix 1: Continued

Date	US	UK	Europe	Others
7-Mar-08	The Federal Reserve increases the size of its Term Auction Facility (TAF) to USD100 billion and extends the maturity of its repos to up to one month.			
11-Mar-08	The Federal Reserve introduces the Term Securities Lending Facility (TSLF), which allows primary dealers to borrow up to USD200 billion of Treasury securities against collateral.		The existing dollar swap arrangements between the Federal Reserve and the ECB and the SNB are increased from a total of USD24 billion to USD36 billion.	
14-Mar-08	On 14 March, 2008, JP Morgan Chase, in conjunction with the Federal Reserve Bank of New York, agreed to provide (under terms and conditions to be agreed) a (up to) 28-day emergency loan to Bear Stearns in order to prevent the potential market crash that would result from Bear Stearns becoming insolvent.			

(Continued)

Appendix 1: Continued

Date	US	UK	Europe	Others
14-Mar-08 (Continued)	Bear Stearns was later acquired by JP Morgan for a consideration of USD1.2 billion or (USD10 per share, up from an initial offer of USD2 per share or consideration of USD240 million), a price far below its 52-week high for the stock of USD133 per share. The acquisition was agreed upon by JP Morgan only after the Fed agreed to assume some of Bear Stearns' most toxic assets, including its holdings of some Countrywide securities, which the Fed assumed as part of its Maiden Lane portfolio. Bear Stearns was the fifth-largest investment bank in the US. At the end of fiscal 2007, Bear Stearns had a net equity position of only USD11.1 billion and USD395 billion in assets, indicating a leverage ratio of 35.5 to 1.			

Appendix 1: Continued

Date	US	UK	Europe	Others
16-Mar-08	The Federal Reserve introduces the Primary Dealer Credit Facility (PDCF), which provides overnight funding for primary dealers in exchange for collateral. The Federal Reserve also lowers the spread between the discount rate and the federal funds rate from 50 to 25 basis points, and lengthens the maximum maturity from 30 to 90 days.			
28-Mar-08			The ECB announces that the maturity of its longer-term refinancing operations (LTROs) would be extended from up to three months to a maximum of six months.	
21-Apr-08		The Bank of England introduces the Special Liquidity Scheme, under which banks can swap illiquid assets for Treasury bills.		

(Continued)

Appendix 1: Continued

Date	US	UK	Europe	Others
2-May-08	The Federal Reserve boosts the size of its TAF programme to USD150 billion, and announces a broadening of the collateral eligible for the TSLF auctions.		The dollar swap arrangements with the ECB and the SNB are increased further, from USD36 billion to USD62 billion.	
Sept.-08			Iceland's Glitner Bank nationalized. Landsbanki and Kaupthing, the two other large banks in Iceland, go into receivership. The three banks collectively had assets of 95 billion euros as of the second quarter of 2008, **11.2x** Iceland's GDP of 8.5 billion euros in 2007. Iceland's foreign debt amounted to 50 billion euros, of which banks captured more than 40 billion euros. Iceland has since requested a USD2 billion from the IMF and a USD4 billion from the Nordic countries.	Russia: the government lends the country's three biggest banks, Sberbank, VTB Bank and Gazprombank, 1.13 trillion rubles (USD44 billion) for at least three months to boost liquidity; the Central Bank lowers the reserve requirement. This is followed by Central Bank loans to keep the current accounts afloat and prevent a bank run and raising the cap for deposit insurance from 400,000 to 700,000 rubles (equivalent to USD25,000).

Appendix 1: Continued

Date	US	UK	Europe	Others
7-Sep-08	Two US Mortgage finance agencies (Fannie Mae and Freddie Mac) are taken into conservatorship.			
14-Sep-08	Federal Reserve expands eligible collateral for Primary Dealer Credit Facility and Term Securities Lending Facility (TSLF), increases frequency and size of schedule 2 TSLF auctions and size of schedule 2 TSLF auctions and eases restrictions on transactions between banks and broker-dealers.			
15-Sep-08	US extends USD70 billion in overnight repos.	UK extends EGP5 billion two-day repos.	ECB extends 30 billion euro overnight repos.	Other central banks provide liquidity, including Japan (Y1.5 trillion) and Australia (AUSD2.1 billion), among others.
15-Sep-08	Lehman Brothers Holdings Inc files for Chapter 11 bankruptcy protection.			

(Continued)

Appendix 1: Continued

Date	US	UK	Europe	Others
16-Sep-08	Reserve Primary Fund, a US money market fund with more than USD50 billion in assets, 'breaks the buck', triggering large volumes of fund redemptions and contagion effects across money and short-term credit markets; the US government steps in to rescue insurance company AIG by extending a USD85 billion two-year credit line to AIG. USD20 billion in 28 day repos.	BoE GBP20 billion two-day and GBP5 billion three-month repos.	ECB extends 70 billion euros overnight repos.	Other central banks provide liquidity including Japan (Y2.5 trillion), Switzerland (SF726.4 million) and Australia (AUSD1.7 billion), among others.
16-Sep-08	AIG ratings downgraded below "AA" levels, US Federal Reserve Bank creates a USD85 billion credit facility to enable the company to meet increased collateral obligations, in exchange for the issuance of a stock warrant to the Federal Reserve Bank for 79.9% of the equity of AIG.			

Appendix 1: Continued

Date	US	UK	Europe	Others
17-Sep-08	US Treasury announces supplemental financing program for Federal Reserve and auctions USD40 billion special cash management bills.	Bank of England (BoE) extends Special Liquidity Scheme.	ECB extends €150 billion 7-day repos.	Other central banks provide liquidity, including Japan (Y3 trillion) and Australia (AUSD4.3 billion), among others.
18-Sep-08	Federal Reserve expands its temporary reciprocal currency arrangements by USD180 billion with major central banks and conducts USD5.0 billion 14-day an USD100 billion overnight repos; Treasury auctions USD60 billion for supplemental financing program,	BoE USD14 billion overnight and GBP66 billion seven-day repos.	ECB: €25 billion overnight and USD40 billion overnight repos	Other central banks provide liquidity, including Japan (Y2.5 trillion), Switzerland (USD10 billion) and Australia (AUSD2.8 billion), among others.
18-Sep-08	New round of coordinated central bank measures address the squeeze in US dollar funding with USD160 billion in new or expanded swap lines.	UK bank HBOS announces its merger with rival Lloyds TSB, UK authorities prohibit short selling of financial shares.		

(Continued)

Appendix 1: Continued

Date	US	UK	Europe	Others
19-Sep-08	The US Treasury announces a temporary guarantee for money market fund investors; the SEC announces a ban on short sales in financial shares; early details emerge of a USD 700 billion US Treasury proposal to remove troubled assets from bank balance sheets (The Troubled Assets Relief Program, TARP).	FSA tightens restrictions on net short positions on financial stocks; BoE conducts USD21 billion in three-day repos.	USD40 billion in three-day repos by the ECB.	
19-Sep-08				Other central banks provide liquidity, including Japan (Y3 trillion), Switzerland (USD10 billion) and Australia (AUSD1.9 billion); among others; several regulatory institutions impose restrictions on equity short sales.
22-Sep-08	Fed conducts USD20 billion in overnight repos.	BoE conducts USD26 billion repos.	ECB conducts USD25 billion 28-day repos.	

Appendix 1: Continued

Date	US	UK	Europe	Others
	On September 22, 2008, the last two major unregulated investment banks in the US, Morgan Stanley and Goldman Sachs, both announced that they would become traditional bank holding companies regulated by the Federal Reserve.			
23-Sep-08	Fed conducts USD20 billion in 28-day repos.	BoE conducts USD30 billion repos.		
23-Sep-08	Berkshire Hathaway agrees to purchase USD5 billion in Goldman's preferred stock, and also receives warrants to buy another USD5 billion in Goldman's common stock, exercisable for a five-year term. Goldman received USD10 billion preferred stock investment from the US Treasury in October 2008, as part of the Troubled Asset Relief Program (TARP).			

(Continued)

Appendix 1: Continued

Date	US	UK	Europe	Others
24-Sep-08	Fed expands its temporary reciprocal currency arrangements to Australian and Scandinavian central banks; conducts USD25 billion in overnight reverse repos.	BoE conducts USD30 billion repos.	ECB: 50 billion euros 84-day repos.	
25-Sep-08	Fed conducts USD22 billion in overnight reverse repos.	BoE conducts USD35 billion repos.		
26-Sep-08	Fed conducts USD26 billion in three-day reverse repos; purchases USD4.5 billion debt notes.	BoE conducts USD10 billion overnight repos and USD30 billion 7-day repos.		
28-Sep-08		Bradford & Bingley (B&B) nationalized; Santander to pay GBP612 million for B&B's branches and deposits.	Fortis partly taken over by governments of Belgium, Netherlands and Luxembourg via 11.2 billion euro bailout package for 49% ownership stake; Germany organizes a €35 billion credit line for Hypo Real Estate, subsequently raised to USD70 billion (50 billion euros).	
29-Sep-08	Troubled US bank Wachovia is taken over; the proposed TARP is rejected by the US House of Representatives.			

Appendix 1: Continued

Date	US	UK	Europe	Others
29-Sep-08	Fed increases swap lines to foreign central banks from USD290 billion to USD620 billion, increases the size of the 84-day Term Auction Facility (TAF) auctions from USD75 billion to USD25 billion, introduces forward TAF auctions.	BOE conducts USD10 billion repos.		ECB conducts 120 billion euro 38-day repos, Iceland's government takes 75% in Glitzier Bank.
30-Sep-08	Fed conducts USD20 billion 28-day repos.	BoE conducts USD10 billion repos.		ECB conducts 190 billion euro, seven-day repos. Delia receives 6.0 billion euro infusion from Belgian and French governments and main shareholders.
30-Sep-08			Irish government guarantees all deposits, covered bonds, senior and dated subordinated debt of six Irish banks (until September 2010).	
30-Sep-08	Big Three automotive companies in the US, General Motors, Ford and Chrysler, ask for USD50 billion to pay for health care expenses and avoid bankruptcy and ensuing layoffs, and Congress worked out a USD25 billion loan.			

(Continued)

Appendix 1: Continued

Date	US	UK	Europe	Others
1-Oct-08	Federal Reserve conducts USD20 billion overnight reverse repos.	BoE conducts USD7.5 billion overnight repos and USD13.4 billion seven-day repos.		
2-Oct-08	Fed conducts USD25 billion overnight reverse repos.	BoE conducts USD8.9 billion repos.	Greek government guarantees all bank deposits.	Brazilian Central Bank eases reserve requirements.
3-Oct-08	The US Congress approves the revised TARP plan. Treasury authorized to purchase distressed assets; FDIC temporarily allowed to borrow unlimited funds from the Treasury; FDIC deposit insurance temporarily increased from USD100,000 to USD250,000 Fed granted the ability to pay interest on reserves; SEC authorized to suspend mark-to-market accounting rules; Fed conducts USD25 billion three-day reverse repos.			

Appendix 1: Continued

Date	US	UK	Europe	Others
3-Oct-08			ECB to allow more banks to participate in unscheduled cash auctions; Netherlands government purchases Dutch operations of Fortis for 16.8 billion euros; ECB auctions USD50 billion overnight repos and a €194 billion liquidity-absorbing quick tender.	
3-Oct-08		BoE extends eligible collateral for its weekly long-term repo operations to include AAA-rated ABS and highly rated ABCP; conducts USD8.2 billion overnight repos and USD30 billion 7-day repos.		
3-Oct-08				Russian Central Bank extends unsecured loans to qualified banks for up to six months and introduces other measures.
7-Oct-08	The US Federal Reserve announces the creation of a new Commercial Paper Funding Facility aimed at buying three-month unsecured and asset-backed commercial paper.			

(Continued)

Appendix 1: Continued

Date	US	UK	Europe	Others
8-Oct-08	US Fed and other major central banks undertake a coordinated round of policy rate cuts.	BoE and major central banks undertake a coordinated round of policy rate cuts.	ECB and major central banks undertake a coordinated round of policy rate cuts.	China, Switzerland, Canada and Sweden along with major central banks undertake a coordinated round of policy rate cuts.
8-Oct-08		UK authorities announce a comprehensive support package, including capital injections for UK-incorporated banks and guarantees for new short- to medium-term senior unsecured bank debt. The plan provides for several sources of funding to be made available, to an aggregate total of GBP500 billion in loans and guarantees. Most simply, GBP200 billion will be made available for short terms loans through the Bank of England's Special Liquidity Scheme. Secondly, the Government will support British banks in their plan to increase their market capitalization through the newly formed		

Appendix 1: Continued

Date	US	UK	Europe	Others
8-Oct-08		Bank Recapitalization Fund, by GBP25 billion in the first instance with a further GBP25 billion to be called upon if needed. Thirdly, the Government will temporarily underwrite any eligible lending between British banks, giving a loan guarantee of around GBP250 billion. However, only GBP400 billion of this is 'fresh money', as there is already in place a system for short term loans to the value of GBP100 billion. All banks incorporated in the UK and building societies are eligible to access the programme.		
13-Oct-08	Major central banks jointly announce measures to improve liquidity in short-term US dollar fund markets, supported by uncapped US dollar swap lines between the Federal Reserve and the other central banks.	Bank of England swaps agreement with Fed to improve USD liquidity.	ECB swaps agreement with Fed to improve USD liquidity.	

(Continued)

Appendix 1: Continued

Date	US	UK	Europe	Others
13-Oct-08			Eurozone governments pledge system-wide bank recapitalizations and guarantees for new bank debt.	
14-Oct-08	The US government announces that up to USD250 billion of previously approved TARP funds are to be used to recapitalize banks; nine large US banks agree to public recapitalization.			
21-Oct-08	The US Federal Reserve announces the creation of a new Money Market Investor Funding Facility, under which it will finance the purchase of short-term debt from money market funds.			
28-Oct-08			Hungary secures a USD25 billion support package from the IMF and other multilateral institutions aimed at stemming growing capital outflows and related currency pressures.	

Appendix 1: Continued

Date	US	UK	Europe	Others
29-Oct-08	To counter the spread of difficulties in obtaining US dollar funding, the US Federal Reserve establishes US dollar swap lines with the monetary authorities in Brazil, Korea, Mexico and Singapore.			To counter the spread of difficulties in obtaining US dollar funding, the US Federal Reserve establishes US dollar swap lines with the monetary authorities in Brazil, Korea, Mexico and Singapore.
12-Nov-08	The US Treasury announces that TARP funds previously earmarked for the purchase of troubled assets will be reallocated to support consumer credit.			
17-Nov-08				Russia: Misprice interbank interest rate on ruble loans reaches a record high of 22.67%, indicating another shortage of liquid funds. Regulator shuts down nine banks.
23-Nov-08	The US government agrees to protect USD306 billion worth of loans and securities on Citigroup's books and to inject USD20 billion of cash in return for a USD27 billion preferred equity stake.		IMF approves standby loan agreement for the Ukraine of USD16.5 billion.	

(Continued)

Appendix 1: Continued

Date	US	UK	Europe	Others
25-Nov-08	The US Federal Reserve announces the creation of a USD200 billion facility to extend loans against securitisations backed by consumer and small business loans; under another programme, up to USD500 billion will be used for purchases of bonds and mortgage-backed securities issued by Fannie Mae, Freddie Mac and the Federal Home Loan Banks.			Russia: S&P Russia's foreign currency credit ratings to BBB (long term), after a negative outlook in October.
8-Dec-08				
8-Jan-09			German lender Commerzbank receives a bailout package to backstop losses at newly acquired Dresdner Bank; the German government takes a 25% stake in the combined entity.	

Appendix 1: Continued

Date	US	UK	Europe	Others
16-Jan-09	Citigroup posts an USD8 billion loss. Replicating an approach taken in the case of Citigroup, the US authorities agree to invest USD20 billion in Bank of America through a preferred equity stake along with guarantees for a pool of USD118 billion of the bank's assets. The measure follows the bank's acquisition of Merrill Lynch earlier in the month.			The Irish authorities seize control of Anglo Irish Bank.
19-Jan-09		Following 2008 losses of about GBP28 billion at the Royal Bank of Scotland, authorities increase their equity stake in the troubled institution to up to 70%. The move forms part of a further broad-based financial rescue package announced on the same day, which includes the extension of existing guarantees for debt issued by participating banks and offers fee-based protection against losses on asset portfolios of financial institutions.		

(Continued)

Appendix 1: Continued

Date	US	UK	Europe	Others
21-Jan-09			French authorities offer to inject up to 10.5 billion euros into eligible banks.	
26-Jan-09		UK announces it will start Quantitative Easing using the Asset Purchase Facility.	The Dutch authorities grant ING Group a backup facility guaranteeing part of the bank's securitized mortgage portfolio worth USD35 billion.	
29-Jan-09				
10-Feb-09	US authorities announce a new, comprehensive support package for the financial sector. The plan anticipates an expansion of the scope of existing measures by incorporating commercial MBS into the Term Asset-Backed Securities Loan Facility (TALF) and proposes a public-private investment fund of USD0.5–1.0 trillion to purchase troubled assets from banks.		Swiss bank UBS reports a fourth quarter loss of CHF 8.1 billion.	

Appendix 1: Continued

Date	US	UK	Europe	Others
17-Feb-09	President Obama signs into law the American Recovery and Reinvestment Act of 2009 which includes a variety of spending measures and tax cuts intended to promote economic recovery.	Bank of England announces the Asset Repurchase Facility will have a size of up to GBP150 billion.	The Latvian government asks the International Monetary Fund and the European Union for an emergency bailout loan of 7.5 billion euros, while at the same time the government nationalizes Parex Bank, the country's second-largest bank. On concerns of bankruptcy, Standard & Poors subsequently downgraded Latvia's credit rating to non-investment grade BB+, or "junk", its worst-ever rating. Its rating was put on negative outlook, which indicates a possible further cut. On February 20 the Latvian coalition government headed by Prime Minister Ivars Godmanis collapses.	Canadian Minister of Finance announces the Government will purchase up to an additional CAD50 billion of insured mortgage pools by the end of the fiscal year as part of its ongoing efforts to maintain the availability of longer-term credit in Canada. This action will increase to CAD75 billion the maximum value of securities purchased through Canada Mortgage and Housing Corporation (CMHC) under this program. Also, the Government will reduce the base commercial pricing of the Canadian Lenders Assurance Facility by 25 basis points. It will also waive the 25 basis point across-the-board surcharge for insurance provided under the Facility until further notice. The Office of the Superintendent of Financial Institutions (OSFI) announces an increase in the allowable limit of innovative and preferred shares in Tier 1 capital.

(Continued)

Appendix 1: Continued

Date	US	UK	Europe	Others
21-Feb-09		UK Banking Act of 2009 comes into effect implementing the Special Resolution Regime (SPR) and replaces temporary powers provided by the Banking (Special Provisions) Act 2008.		
23-Feb-09		UK Government announces plans for Northern Rock to increase mortgage lending by up to GBP14 billion over the next two years.		
26-Feb-09		RBS announces an attributable loss of GBP24.1 billion. UK Government announces details of an Asset Protection Scheme (APS) and an agreement in principle with RBS to participate in the APS, including increased lending commitments.		
27-Feb-09	US Treasury announces its willingness to convert up to USD25 billion of Citigroup preferred stock issued under the Capital Purchase Program (CPP) into common equity, a 36% equity stake.	Lloyds announces results, including a pre-tax loss of GBP10.8 billion for HBOS.		

Appendix 1: Continued

Date	US	UK	Europe	Others
2-Mar-09	US authorities announce a restructuring of their assistance to AIG. Under the restructuring, AIG will receive as much as USD30 billion of additional capital.	HSBC announces plans to raise GBP12.5 billion in a rights issue.		
3-Mar-09	US authorities announce the launch of the Term Asset Backed Securities Loan Facility (TALF) where the Federal Reserve Bank of New York will lend up to USD200 billion to eligible owners of certain AAA-rated asset-backed securities.			
5-Mar-09		Bank of England reduces Bank Rate by 50 bps to 0.5% and announces a GBP75 billion quantitative easing mechanism.		
7-Mar-09		UK Government announces an agreement in principle with Lloyd's to participate in the APS, including additional lending commitments.		

(Continued)

Appendix 1: Continued

Date	US	UK	Europe	Others
18-Mar-09	Federal Reserve maintains the effective federal funds rate at 0% to 0.25% and announces an expansion of over USD1 trillion in its planned asset purchases in 2009.			
19-Mar-09		Bank of England publishes details of its Corporate Bond Secondary Market Scheme as part of its Asset Purchase Facility (APF).		
20-Mar-09		FSA confirms Scarborough Building Society merger with the Skipton Building Society.		
23-Mar-09	US Treasury announces details on the Public-Private Investment Program for Legacy Assets. The Treasury will provide 50% of the equity capital.			
24-Mar-09	IMF creates the Flexible Credit Line (FCL), inviting applications from strong-performing countries.			

Appendix 1: Continued

Date	US	UK	Europe	Others
29-Mar-09			Spanish Central Bank saves Caja Castilla La Mancha with a nine billion euro bailout package after it faced liquidity problems.	
30-Mar-09			Standard & Poor's (S&P) lowers the long-term sovereign credit rating of Ireland from AAA to AA+, with a negative outlook.	
30-Mar-09		Bank of England announces that key parts of Dunfermline Building Society have been transferred to Nationwide Building Society under the Special Resolution Regime (SRR).		
2-Apr-09	G20 Summit communiqué announces a trebling of the IMF's available resources to USD750 billion.			
7-Apr-09			Irish Government announces plans for the National Asset Management Agency to manage the worst-performing land and development loans of Irish banks.	

(Continued)

Appendix 1: Continued

Date	US	UK	Europe	Others
9-Apr-09		CVC Capital Partners agrees to buy shares from Barclays for GBP3.0 billion.	German Government begins the process to take over Hypo Real Estate.	
17-Apr-09				IMF approves a USD47 billion credit line for Mexico under the new FCL.
22-Apr-09		UK Government launches Asset-backed Securities Guarantee Scheme, under which HM Treasury will provide credit guarantees and liquidity guarantees on residential mortgage-backed securities issued by UK banks and building societies.		
6-May-09				IMF approves a USD20.6 billion credit line for Poland under the IMF's new FCL.
7-May-09	Federal Reserve releases the results of the 'stress test' of the 19 largest US bank holding companies. The assessment finds that losses at the 19 firms during 2009 and 2010 could be USD600 billion and ten firms would need to add, in aggregate, USD185 billion to their capital to maintain buffers to hedge against adverse economic scenarios.	Bank of England maintains Bank Rate at 0.5% and increases the size of the asset purchase programme by GBP50 billion to GBP125 billion.	ECB announces it will lower its policy rate to 1%. This comes after a reduction of 50 bps in March and 25 bps in April. It expects to purchase around 60 billion euros worth of covered bonds, and the European Investment Bank (EIB) will become an eligible counterparty in the Eurosystem's monetary policy operations.	

Appendix 1: Continued

Date	US	UK	Europe	Others
21-May-09		S&P affirms the long-term sovereign credit rating of the UK, but revises the outlook to negative.		
23-May-09	The Federal Reserve Bank and the US Treasury had increased potential financial support to AIG, with the support of an investment of as much as USD70 billion, a USD60 billion credit line and USD52.5 billion to buy mortgage-based assets owned or guaranteed by AIG, increasing the total amount available to as much as USD182.5 billion.			
1-Jun-09	Chrysler and General Motors Corporation and its three domestic subsidiaries announce filing for relief under Chapter 11 of the US Bankruptcy Code.		The Ukrainian state becomes the de-facto owner of Ukrhazbank (84.21% after investing UAH 3.2 billion), Rodovid Bank (99.97% after investing UAH 2.809 billion) and Bank Kyiv (99.93% after investing UAH 3.563 billion) in May and early June 2009.	

(Continued)

Appendix 1: Continued

Date	US	UK	Europe	Others
8-Jun-09				S&P lowers the long-term sovereign credit rating of Ireland from AA+ to AA, with a negative outlook.
9-Jun-09	US Treasury announces that the largest US financial institutions participating in the CPP have met the requirements for repayment.			
11-Jun-09	BlackRock agrees to pay USD13.5 billion to buy Barclays Global Investors.			
12-Jun-09		West Bromwich Building Society announces strengthening its core Tier 1 capital position by swapping subordinated debt for a new instruments which will qualify as core Tier 1 capital.		
17-Jun-09	President Obama announces a comprehensive plan for regulatory reform. The plan would give the Federal Reserve new responsibilities for consolidated supervision of systemically important banks among other challenges.			

Appendix 1: Continued

Date	US	UK	Europe	Others
17-Jun-09	U.S. Bancorp and **BB&T** become the first large financial institutions to announce it has repaid the government in full for the preferred shares it bought last fall under the federal bailout program.			
19-Jun-09	USD68 billion in TARP repayments by Morgan Stanley; Goldman Sachs, Bank of New York Mellon, JP Morgan, American Express, State Street Corporation, US Bancorp and Northern Trust.			
20-Jun-09			The ECB starts to provide liquidity through longer-term refinancing operations (LTROs) with a maturity of one year. The operations have been conducted as fixed rate tender procedures with full allotment and have been in addition to the regular and supplementary LTROs.	

(Continued)

Appendix 1: Continued

Date	US	UK	Europe	Others
25-Jun-09	The former finance arm of General Motors, GMAC, which had around a third of its assets allocated to mortgage finance through Residential Capital, known as ResCap, is bailed out by the US government over the course of 2009 with injections of more than USD16 billion.			
6-Aug-09		Bank of England increases Asset Purchase Facility to GBP175 billion.		
17-Sep-09			World Bank approves a loan for Ukraine in the amount of USD400 million.	
Oct-09			Since the October elections, Greece has been in a state of crisis after the new Government restated the budget deficit to 12.7% of GDP. Greece's public debt is expected to rise this year from 113% to more than 120% of GDP. The costs of insuring against a default on debt have risen to the highest	

Appendix 1: Continued

Date	US	UK	Europe	Others
Oct-09			levels in six years since the market was launched — or USD340,000 for every USD10 million of debt annually over five years. The new Greek Government's plan to cut the budget deficit from nearly 13 percent to under 3 percent in three years sounds implausible. That implies that Greece would, in one coherent sweep, push through profound reforms of the public and private sectors that it has not yet been able to tackle. The threat of a Greek default may matter even more to the Eurozone than it does to Greece itself. If Greece defaults, other countries with high debt will all face dramatically higher borrowing costs. A Greek default immediately mean a challenge to Portugal, Spain and Italy.	

(Continued)

Appendix 1: Continued

Date	US	UK	Europe	Others
2-Nov-09	CIT group, a large US commercial and consumer finance company, files for bankruptcy after the USD3.0 billion loan it securitized on July 20, 2009, from bondholders failed to be sufficient to prevent it.			
30-Nov-09				Dubai World, a real estate holding company with operations in more than 100 countries and debts in excess of USD59 billion, announces it wants to delay payments on some USD26 billion owed to creditors, including HSBC and Standard Chartered Bank.
3-Dec-09			On 3 December 2009, the ECB announces that it would discontinue this programme, allotting its last 12-month LTRO on 16 December 2009. In addition, the ECB decided to stop its six-month LTROs in the if rest quarter of 2010, by carrying out the last operation on 31 March.	

Appendix 1: Continued

Date	US	UK	Europe	Others
14-Dec-09	Citigroup announces it will repay USD20 billion to exit TARP programme. Wells Fargo and FITB remain part of the TARP programme.			On December 14, 2009 the Dubai government receives USD10 billion in surprise aid from Abu Dhabi for debt-laden Dubai World, which said it would use USD4.1 billion of it to repay its Nakheel unit's Islamic bond maturing on the same day.

Sources: Bloomberg, Bank of England, Federal Reserve Board, ECB Financial Stability Report, Bloomberg, FT, WSJ, BIS Quarterly Reviews, IMF GFSR various issues 2007, 2008 and 2009. Wikipedia.

Appendix 2

A BRIEF HISTORY OF CRISES
IN THE PAST

Appendix 2

		DD (2005)	KR (1999)	CK (1996)	CK (2003)	RR (2008)	LV (2008)	Consolidated
1	Australia			1989–1990	1989–1992	1989		**1989–1992**
2	Austria							
3	Belgium							
4	Canada				1983–1985			**1983–85**
5	Czech Republic							
6	Denmark		1987–1990		1987–1992	1987		**1987–1992**
7	Finland	1991–94	1991–92	1991–93	1991–94	1992	1991–93	**1991–94**
8	France			1994–95	1994–95	1994		**1994–95**
9	Germany			1970s	Late 1970s	1977		**1975–77**
10	Greece				1991–95	1992		**1991–95**
11	Hungary							
12	Iceland				1985–86, 1993		1975, 81, 89	**1975, 1981, 85, 86, 89, 93**
13	Ireland							
14	Italy	1990–95			1990–95	1990	1981	**1981, 1990–95**
15	Japan	1992–2002 , 2005		1990s	1990s	1992	1997	**1992–2002, 2005**
16	Korea	1997–2002			1997–2002		1997–98	**1997–98**
17	Luxembourg							
18	Mexico	1982, 1994–97	1982–84	1981 to 1982, 1995	1981–91, 1994–2000	1980–83, 1994	1977, 81, 82, 94, 95	**1977, 81–91, 94–2000**

19 Netherlands						
20 Norway	1987–93	1987–89	1990–93	1987	1991	**1987–1993**
21 New Zealand		1987–90	1987–90	1987	1987	**1987–1990**
22 Poland		1990–93	1992–95	1989–93	1981, 1992	**1981, 1989–95**
23 Portugal	1986–89				1983	**1983, 1986–89**
24 Slovakia						
25 Spain	1978–83	1977–85	1977–85	1977	1977, 83	**1977–85**
26 Sweden	1990–93	1991	1991–94	1992	1992	**1990–94**
27 Switzerland						
28 Turkey	1982, 1991, 1994, 2000–02, 2005	1982–85	1982–85, 1994, 2000	1980–83, 1994	1978, 82, 84, 91, 96, 2000, 2001	**1978–85, 91, 94, 96, 2000–02, 2005**
29 UK		1974–76	1974–76, 1984, 1991, 1995	1984, 1992, 1995	2007	**1974–76, 84, 91, 92, 95, 2007**
30 US	1980–1992	1984–91	1988–91	1974, 1984, 2007	1988, 2007	**1974, 1980–92, 2007**

Key:

DD (2005): Demirgüç-Kunt & Enrica Detragiache (2005).
KR (1999): Kaminsky & Reinhart (1999).
CK: Caprio & Klingebiel (1996 and 2003).
RR (2008): Reinhart & Rogoff (2008).
LV (2008) Laeven & Valencia (2008).

REFERENCES

"Early Warning System Models: The Next Steps Forward." IMF Global Financial Stability Report, Chapter IV, 2002.

"Stress and Deleveraging Macro-financial Implications and Policy." IMF Global Financial Stability Report. October 2008.

"The State of Public Finances: Outlook and Medium-Term Policies After the 2008 Crises." Fiscal Affairs Department, IMF, March 6, 2009.

"The Turner Review: A Regulatory Response to the Global Banking Crisis. FSA. March, 2009.

Abiad, Abdul. "Early Warning Systems: A Survey and a Regime-Switching Approach." IMF Working Paper WP/03/32, 2003.

Abiad, Abdul, Enrica Detragiache, and Thierry Tressel. "A New Database of Financial Reforms." IMF Working Paper. WP/08/266, 2008.

Acharya, Viral V., and Mathew Richardson (eds). *Restoring Financial Stability, How to Repair a Failed System.* John Wiley and Sons. 2009.

Akerlof, G. P. and Romer, P. "Looting: the economic underworld of bankruptcy for profit." *Brookings Papers on Economic Activity*, pp.1–73, 1993.

Alessi, Lucia (European Central Bank) and Carsten Dektken (European Central Bank), 'Real Time' Early Warning Indicators for Costly Asset Price Boom/Bust Cycles: A Role for Global Liquidity? CREI (Universitat Pompeu Fabra), Barcelona, 21–23 November 2008.

Andreou, Irène, Gilles Dufrénot, Alain Sand and Aleksandra Zdzienicka. "A Forewarning Indicator System for Financial Crises: The Case of Six Central and Eastern European Countries (April 2007)." William Davidson Institute Working Paper No. 901; GATE Working Paper No. 07–09. Available at SSRN: http://ssrn.com/abstract=988071, 2008.

Barrell, Ray. "The Great Crash of 2008." *National Institute Economic Review* no. 206, October 2008.

Barrell, Ray and E. Philip Davis. "The Evolution of the Financial Crisis of 2007/2008." *National Institute Economic Review* no. 206, October 2008.

Barrell, Ray, Ian Hurst and Simon Kirby. "Financial Crises, Regulation and Growth." *National Institute Economic Review*. October 2008 206: 56–65, DOI:10.1177/0027950108099843.

Barth, James R., Gerard Caprio Jr. and Ross Levine. "Bank Regulation and Supervision: What Works Best." *Journal of Financial Intermediation*, 13 (2004) 205–48.

Bell, J and Darren Pain. Leading Indicator Models of Banking Crises – A Critical Review." *Financial Stability Review*. Bank of England, issue 9, article 3, pp. 113–29, 2000.

Berg, Andrew, Eduardo Borensztein, and Catherine Pattillo. "Assessing Early Warning Systems: How Have They Worked in Practice?" IMF Working Paper. WP/04/52, 2004.

Bhattacharyay, Biswa N. "Towards a Macro-Prudential Leading Indicators Framework for Monitoring Financial Vulnerability (August 2003)." CESifo Working Paper Series no. 1015.

Bordo, M., B. Eichengreen, D. Klingebiel and M. S. Marinez-Peria. "Financial Crises: Lessons from the last 120 Years." *Economic Policy.* April, 2001.

Borio, Claudio and Mathias Drehmann. "Assessing the Risk of Banking Crises Revisited." *BIS Quarterly Review*, March 2009.

Borio, Claudio and P. McGuire. "The Macroprudential Approach to Regulation and Supervision: Where Do We Stand?" *Kredittilsynet* special 20th anniversary volume, 2006.

Ibid. "Twin Peaks in Equity and Housing Prices?" *BIS Quarterly Review*, March 2004.

Borio, Claudio and Philip Lowe. "Assessing the Risk of Banking Crises." *BIS Quarterly Review*, December 2002.

Borio, Claudio, and Mathias Drehmann. Towards an Operational Framework for Financial Stability: 'Fuzzy' Measurement and its Consequences." Twelfth Annual Conference of the Banco de Chile. 'Financial Stability Monetary Policy and Central Banking, Santiago, 6–7 November 2008.

Boss, Michael, Gerald Krenn, Claus Puhr and Martin Summer, "Systemic Risk Monitor: A Model for Systemic Risk Analysis and Stress Testing of Banking Systems." Financial Stability Report, Oesterreichische Nationalbank (Austrian Central Bank), issue 11, pp. 83–95, June, 2006.

Breuer, J.B. "An Exegesis on Currency and Banking Crises." *Journal of Economic Surveys*, vol. 18, pp 293–320, 2004.

Buiter, Willem H. and Anne Slbert. "The Icelandic Banking Crisis and What to Do about It: The Lender of Last Resort Theory of Optimal Currency Areas." *CEPR Policy Insight* no. 26, October 2008.

Bussiere, Mathieu and Marcel Fratzscher. "Towards a New Early Warning System for Financial Crises." ECB Working Paper No. 145, May 2002.

Canbas, Serpil, Yildrim B. Onal, Hatice G. Duzakin and Suleyman B. Kilic. "Prediction of Financial Distress by Multi-Variate Statistical Analysis: The Case of Firms Taken into the Surveillance Market in the Istanbul Stock Exchange." *International Journal of Theoretical and Applied Finance*, vol. 9, no. 1 (2006) 133–50. World Scientific Publishing, June 2005.

Caprio, Gerard Jr., and Daniela Klingebiel. "Episodes of Systemic and Borderline Financial Crises." World Bank Research Data Set, 2003.

Caprio, Gerard Jr., and Klingebiel. "Bank Insolvencies: Cross-country Experience." World Bank Policy Research Working Paper No. 1620, 1996.

Central Bank of Egypt. Macroprudential Unit Brief, Issue 10, 26 July, 2007.

Central Bank of Egypt. Macroprudential Unit Brief, Issue 12, 9 August, 2007.

Central Bank of Egypt. Macroprudential Unit Brief, Issue 16, 1 October , 2007.

Central Bank of Egypt. Macroprudential Unit Brief, Issue 17, 17 October, 2007.

Central Bank of Egypt. Macroprudential Unit Brief, Issue 20, 28 November, 2007.

Central Bank of Egypt. Macroprudential Unit Brief, Issue 21, 25 December, 2007.

Central Bank of Egypt. Macroprudential Unit Brief, Issue 25, 2 March, 2008.

Central Bank of Egypt. Macroprudential Unit Brief, Issue 26, 19 March, 2008.

Chan, Jorge A. and Toni Gravelle. "The END: A New Indicator of Financial and Non-Financial Corporate Sector Vulnerability." IMF Working Paper, WP/05/231, December 2005.

Chang, Roberto and A. Velasco. "Financial Crises in Emerging Markets: A Canonical Model." NBER Working Paper 6606, Boston, MA, 1998.

Chen, Yu-Fu, Michael Funke and Kadri Mannasoo. "Extracting Leading Indicators of Bank Fragility from Market Prices. "CESifo Working Paper No. 1647, Category 6, Monetary Policy and International Finance, 2006.

Cihak, Martin. "Systemic Loss: A Measure of Financial Stability." *Czech Journal of Economics & Finance*, 57 (1–2), 2007.

Cihak, Martin and Klaus Shaeck. "How Well Do Aggregate Bank Ratios Identify Banking Problems?" IMF Working Paper, WP/07/275, 2007.

Claessens, Stijn, Daniela Klingebiel and Luc Laeven. "Resolving Systemic Financial Crises: Policies and Institutions." World Bank Policy Research Working Paper 3377, August 2004.

Curry, Timothy J., Peter J. Elmer and Gary S. Fissel. "Can Equity Markets Help Predict Bank Failure?" FDIC Working Paper, July 2004.

Danielsson, Jon. "The First Casualty of the Crisis: Iceland." VOX, November, 2008.

Davis, E. Philip and Dilruba Karim. "Could Early Warning Systems Have Helped to Predict the Sub-Prime Crisis?" *National Institute Economic Review*, 2008.

Ibid. "Comparing Early Warning Systems for Banking Crises." *Journal of Financial Stability*, vol. 4, June 2008. pp 89–120.

Dell'Ariccia, Giovanni, Enrica Detragiacheand Raghuram Rajan. "The Real Effect of Banking Crises." *Journal of Financial Intermediation*. 25 August 2007.

Demirguc-Kunt, Asli, and Enrica Detragiache. "The Determinants of Banking Crises in Developing and Developed Countries." IMF Staff Papers, vol. 45, pp 81–109, 1998.

Ibid. "Cross-Country Empirical Studies of Systemic Bank Distress: A Survey." IMF Working Paper WP/05/96, 2005.

Ibid. "Monitoring Banking Sector Fragility: A Multivariate Logit Approach with An Application to the 1996/97 Banking Crises." *World Bank Economic Review*, vol. 14, No. 2, pp. 287–307, 2000.

Demirguc-Kunt, Asli and Enrica Detragiache, and Poonam Gupta. "Inside the Crisis: An Empirical Analysis of Banking Systems in Distress." IMF Working Paper No. 00/156, 2000.

Dooley, Michael P. "A Model of Crises in Emerging Markets." *The Economic Journal*, 2000.

Drees, Burkhard and Ceyla Pazarbasioglu. "The Nordic Banking Crisis: Pitfalls in Financial Liberalization." IMF Working Paper, 1995.

Dumtrescu, Cornelia Tomescu. "The Factors that Determine the Financial Crises and the Possibilities in Which they Can be Anticipated and Prevented." Constantin Brancusi University of Targu Jiu Working Paper Series.

Duttagupta, Rupa and Paul Cashin. "The Anatomy of Banking Crises." IMF Working Paper, WP/08/93, April 2008.

Eichengreen, B. and C. Arteta. "Banking Crises in Emerging Markets: Presumptions and Evidence." Center for International and Development Economic Research Working Paper, C00–115, August, 2000.

Eichengreen, B. and A. K. Rose. "Staying Afloat When the Wind Shifts: External Factors and Emerging-Market Banking Crises." CEPR Discussion Paper, 1998.

Freedman, Charles Michael Kumhof, Douglas Lazton and Jaewoo Lee. "The Case for Global Fiscal Stimulus." IMF Staff Position Note, 6 March, 2009.

Gaytan, Alejandro and Christian A. Johnson. "A Review of the Literature on Early Warning Systems for Banking Crises." Working Paper No. 183. Central Bank of Chile, 2002.

Ghosh, Swati and Atish Ghosh. "Structural Vulnerabilities and Currency Crises." IMF Working Paper, 2002.

Gieve, John. Seven Lessons from the Last Three Years. Speech at LSE, February 19, 2009.

Gilmore, Grainne. "Toxic Debts Could Reach USD4.0 trillion." *The Times Online*. April 7, 2009.

Global Development Finance Report. World Bank, 2008.

Godlewski, Christophe J. "Regulatory and Institutional Determinants of Credit Risk Taking and a Bank's Default in Emerging Market Economies: A Two-Step Approach." *Journal of Emerging Market Finance*, 2006.

Goodhart, Charles. "The Boundary Problem in Financial Regulation." *National Institute Economic Review*. October 2008, 206: 48–55, DOI: 10.1177/0027950108099842.

Goodhart, Charles, Lea Zicchino, Dimitrios Tsomocos, Miguel Segoviano and Oriol Aspachs Bracon. "Searching for a Metric for Financial Stability." FMG Special Papers sp167, Financial Markets Group, 2006.

Gonzalez-Hermosillo, Brenda. "Determinants of Ex-Ante Banking System Distress: A Macro-Micro Empirical Exploration of Some Recent Episodes." IMF Working Paper, wp/99/33, 1999.

Gourinchas, Pierre-Olivier, Rodrigo Valdes and Oscar Landerretche. "Lending Booms: Latin America and the World." NBER Working Paper 8249, 2001.

Gropp, Reint, Jukka Vesala and Giuseppe Vulpes. "Equity and Bond Market Signals as Leading Indicators of Bank Fragility." *Journal of Money, Credit and Banking*, 2004.

Gunther, Jeffrey W., Robert R. Moore. "Early Warning Models in Real Time." *Journal of Banking and Finance*, 27, 2003.

Heffernan, Shelagh. *Modern Banking*. John Wiley and Sons, 2004.

Haldane, Andrew, Simon Hall and Silvia Pezzini. "A New Approach to Assessing Risks to Financial Stability." Bank of England, Financial Stability Paper No. 2, April 2007.

Hardy, Daniel C. and Ceyla Pazarbasioglu. "Leading Indicators of Banking Crises: Was Asia Different?" IMF Working Paper, WP/98/91, 1998.

Hasmann, R. and L. Rojas Suarez (eds). *The Roots of Banking Crises: The Macroeconomic Context, Banking Crises in Latin America*. Baltimore: Johns Hopkins University Press, pp 27–63, 1996.

Hawkings, John and Marc Klau. "Measuring Potential Vulnerabilities in Emerging Market Economies." *BIS* Working Paper no. 91, October 2000.

Herrera, Santiago and Conrado A. Garcia Corado. "A User's Guide to an Early Warning System for Macroeconomic Vulnerability in Latin American Countries (November 1999)." World Bank Policy Research Working Paper No. 2233, 1999.

Hoggarth, Glenn and Jack Reidhill. "Resolution of Banking Crises: A Review." *Financial Stability Review*. Bank of England, December 2003.

Hoggarth, Glenn, R. Reis and Victoria Saporta. "Costs of banking instability: some empirical evidence." *Journal of Banking and Finance*, Vol. 26, pages 825–855 and Bank of England Working Paper No. 144, 2002.

Holland, Dawn, Ray Barrell, Tatiana Fic. Sylvia Gottschalk, Ian Hurst and Iana Liadze. "The Impact of the Financial Crisis on the Euro Area." *National Institute Economic Review*, no. 206, October 2008.

Honohan, Patrick. "Banking System Failures in Developing and Transition Countries: Diagnosis and Prediction." *BIS* Working Paper 39, January 1997.

Ibid. "Risk Management and the Costs of the Banking Crises." *National Institute Economic Review* no. 206, October 2008.

Horton, Mark and Anna Ivanove. "The Size of the Fiscal Expansion: An Analysis for the Largest Countries." IMF Fiscal Affairs Department, IMF Note, February 2009.

IMF GFSR. April 2008 and October 2008.

Jagtiani, Julapa, James Kolaris, Catharine Lemieux and Hwan Shin. "Early Warning Models for Bank Supervision: Simpler Could be Better." Federal Reserve Bank of Chicago, *Economic Perspectives*, Q3, 2003.

Johnston, R. Barry, Jingqing Chair and Liliana Schumacher. "Assessing Financial System Vulnerabilities." IMF Working Paper, WP/00/76, April 2000.

Kaminsky, Graciela L. "Currency and Banking Crises: The Early Warnings of Distress." International Finance Discussion Paper No. 629, October 1998.

Kaminsky, G. L. and C. M. Reinhart. "The Twin Crises: The Causes of Banking and Balance-of-payments Problems." *American Economic Review*, vol. 89 (3), pp 473–500, 1999.

Kane, E. *The S&L Insurance Mess: How Did it Happen?*. Washington, DC.: Urban Institute Press, 1989.

Kaufman, George G. "Macro-Economic Stability and Bank Soundness." University of Chicago Presentation at the Conference on Financial Reform and Stability, India, sponsored by the IMF, 2001.

King, Thomas B., Daniel A. Nuxoll, and Timothy J. Yeager. "Are the Causes of Bank Distress Changing? Can Researchers Keep Up?" *Federal Reserve Bank of St. Louis Journal*, January/February 2006.

Kolari, James, Michele Caputo and Drew Wagner. "Trait Recognition: An Alternative Approach to EWS in Commercial Banking." *Journal of Business Finance & Accounting*, December 1996.

Krainer, John and Jose A. Lopez. "Incorporating Equity Market Information into Supervisory Monitoring Models." *Journal of Money, Credit & Banking*, 2004.

Laeven, Luc A. and Valencia, Fabian V. "Systemic Banking Crises: A New Database," IMF Working Papers, 2008.

Lall, S., R. Cardarelli and S. Elekdag. "Financial Stress and Economic Downturns." IMF WEO October, 2008, Chapter 4.

Lestano, Jan Jacobs and Gerard H. Kuper, "Indicators of Financial Crises do Work! An Early-Warning System for Six Asian Countries, Department of Economics, University of Groningen." Paper provided by EconWPA in its series International Finance, No. 0409001, 2003.

Lieu, Pang-Tien, Ching-Wen Lin and Hui-Fun Yu. "Financial Early-Warning Models on Cross-Holding Groups, Industrial Management & Data Systems." Vol. 108, no. 8, 2008.

Lindgren, C. J., Garcia, G. and Saal, M. *Bank Soundness and Macroeconomic Policy*. Washington, D.C.: IMF, 1996.

Logan, Andrew. "G10 Seminar on Systems for Assessing Banking System Risk." Bank of England FSR, June 2000.

Ibid. "The United Kingdom's Small Banks' Crisis of the early 1990s: what were the leading indicators of failure?" Bank of England Working Paper, 2001.

Manasse, Paolo and Nouriel Roubini "'Rules of Thumb' for Sovereign Debt Crises." IMF Working Paper, 2005.

Manasse, Paolo, Nouriel Roubini and Axel Schimmelpfennig. "Predicting Sovereign Debt Crises." IMF Working Paper, 2003.

Miles, David and David McCarthy. "Optimal Portfolio Allocation for Corporate Pension Funds." *Morgan Stanley Economics*. November 28, 2007.

Mishkin, Frederic S. "The Household Balance Sheet and the Great Depression." *The Journal of Economic History*, vol. 38, no. 4 (December 1978) pp. 918–37.

Mulder, Christian Roberto Perrelli and Manuel Rocha. "The Role of Corporate, Legal and Macroeconomic Balance Sheet Indicators in Crisis Detection and Prevention." IMF Working Paper, March 2002.

Nier, Erlend W., "Financial Stability Frameworks and the Role of Central Banks: Lessons From the Crisis." IMF Working Paper, 2009.

O'Keefe, John, Virginia Olin and Christopher A. Richardson. "Bank Loan-Underwriting Practices: Can Examiners' Risk Assessments Contribute to Early-Warning Systems?" FDIC Working Paper No. 2003–06, 2003.

Peek, Joe and Eric S. Rosengren. "Will Legislated Early Intervention Prevent the Next Banking Crisis?" Online: SSRN: http://ssrn.com/abstract=173170, 1999.

Poghosyan, Tirgan and Martin Cihak. "Distress in European Banks: An Analysis Based on a New Data Set." IMF Working Paper, WP/09/9, 2009.

Reinhart, Carmen and Andrew Felton. "The First Global Financial Crisis of the 21st Century, Part II: Introduction." VOX, February 2009.

Reinhart, Carmen and Vincent Reinhart. "Capital Flow Bonanzas: An Encompassing View of the Past and Present." CEPR Discussion Paper 6996, October 2008.

Ibid. "From Capital Flow Bonanza to Financial Crash." VOX, October 2008.

Reinhart, Carmen M. and Kenneth S. Rogoff. "This Time is Different: A Panoramic View of Eight Centuries of Financial Crises." Harvard University and University of Maryland Working Paper, April 2008.

Reisen, Helmut. "The Fallout from the Global Credit Crisis: Contagion – Emerging Markets Under Stress." VOX, December 2008.

Rojas-Suarez, Liliana. "Rating Banks in Emerging Markets: What Credit Rating Agencies Should Learn From Financial Indicators." Institute for International Economics Working Paper No. 01–06, 2003.

Rose, Andrew K. and Mark M. Spiegel. Cross-Country Causes and Consequences of the 2008 Crisis: International Linkages and American Exposure. CEPR Discussion Papers no. 7354, September, 2009.

Sachs, Jeffrey D. Aaron Tornell, Andres Velasco, Guillermo A. Calvo and Richard N. Cooper. "Financial Crises in Emerging Markets: The Lessons from 1995." Brookings Papers on Economic Activity, 1996.

Santomero, Anthony M. and Paul Hoffman. "Problem Bank Resolution: Evaluating the Options." Wharton Financial Institutions Center Working Paper, October 1998.

Savona, Roberto and Marika Vezzoli. "Multidimensional Distance to Collapse Point and Sovereign Default Prediction." CAREFIN Research Paper no. 12/08, 2008.

Simpson, John L. "International Banking Risk Scoring During the Asian Debt and Banking Crisis (September 1999)." Curtin U Economics and Finance Working Paper no. 99–11.

Tieman, Alexander, F. and Andrea M. Maechler. The Real Effects of Financial Sector Risk, September 2009. IMF Working Paper, WP/09/198.

Turner, Adair. "Regulating Banks and Markets: Six Theoretical Issues." Presentation by Lord Adair Turner, Chairman, Financial Services Authority (FSA) at Cass Business School, 18 March, 2008.

Van den Berg, Jeroen, Bertrand Candelon and Jean-Pierre Urbain. "A Cautious Note on the Use of Panel Models to Predict Financial Crises." Economic Letters 101 (2008) 80–83.

Wadhwani, Sushil. "Should Monetary Policy Respond to Asset Price Bubbles? Revisiting the Debate." National Institute Economic Review, 2008.

White, William R. "Past Financial Crises, the Current Financial Turmoil, and the Need for a New Macrofinancial Stability Framework." Journal of Financial Stability 4 (2008) 307–12.

Wilmarth, Arthur E., *TOO-BIG-TO-FAIL: POLICIES AND PRACTICES IN GOVERNMENT BAILOUTS*, Benton E. Gup, ed., Quorum Books, Greenwood Publishing Group, 2003.

Wong, Jim, Eric Wong and Phyllis Leung. "A Leading Indicator Model of Banking Distress – Developing an Early Warning System for Hong Kong and Other EMEAP Economies." Hong Kong Monetary Authority, Working Paper 22/2007, 2007.

Wood, Duncan. "Basel Committee to Look at Tier 1 Capital Quality." *Risk Magazine*, 4 March, 2009.

Worrell, DeLisle. "Quantitative Financial Assessment of the Financial Sector: An Integrated Approach." IMF Working Paper, WP/04/153, 2004.

Zicchino, Lea, Dimitrios Tsomocos, Miguel Segoviano, Charles Goodhart and Oriol Aspachs Bracon. "Searching for a Metric for Financial Stability." FMG Special Papers sp167, Financial Markets Group, 2006.

INDEX

Note: Numbers in **boldface** indicate figures.

Lightning Source UK Ltd.
Milton Keynes UK
28 October 2010

161990UK00002B/12/P